A special needs teacher by training and profession, Liz Dorton runs her own puppet theatre company, making, performing and training for Health, Education and Community organizations in her home town of Hull, with a special emphasis on the outer city council estate where she lives. Her puppets vary from shadow and rod to giant figures with a bit of pyrotechnics thrown in.

As part of a local team of children's workers, Liz has developed Christian teaching and activity programmes for children, many of which now form the basis of the CURBS most popular teaching resources, such as *Upside-down kingdom*, *The Beatitudes*, *The three parties* and *Everybody's a somebody*.

Liz enjoys unearthing life issues buried within scripture and making them relevant for children through the arts and the child's own culture, peer group and family experiences within the local context.

Christine Wright is a freelance writer and editor living in Wendover, Buckinghamshire. Trained as a nursery teacher, she created and edited under-fives material for Scripture Union for twelve years, but has worked with children of al ... ere). She enjoys fi ... n to grow in faith ... an imaginative an ... ter story. Using it ... owledge about Jesus' death a ... rrection and will provide an experience that touches the heart and engenders a sense of wonder and awe in response.

Kathryn Copsey (Project Consultant) is the project leader of CURBS (Children in URBan Situations) and author of two books, *Become Like a Child* (SU, 1994) and *From the Ground Up* (BRF, 2005). A trained community worker, she has worked with children for the past 30 years, the majority of which have been in urban situations such as East London. Kathryn is former editor of Scripture Union's SALT programme for 5–7s. She has been part of the authorship team and provided editorial input for all the resources produced under the CURBS umbrella over the past seven years. Kathryn and her husband both live and work in East London and have two grown-up children.

IMPORTANT INFORMATION

Photocopying permission

The Copyright Licensing Agency (CLA)

BRF is a Registered Charity (No. 233280)

Published by
The Bible Reading Fellowship
First Floor, Elsfield Hall
15–17 Elsfield Way, Oxford OX2 8FG
Website: www.brf.org.uk

ISBN 1 84101 387 0
First published 2005
10 9 8 7 6 5 4 3 2 1 0

Acknowledgments
Unless otherwise stated, scripture quotations are taken from the Contemporary English Version of the Bible published by HarperCollins Publishers, copyright © 1991, 1992, 1995 American Bible Society.

A catalogue record for this book is available from the British Library

Printed in Singapore by Craft Print International Ltd

Colours of EASTER

A visual approach to the Easter story using colour, sound and light

Liz Dorton and Christine Wright

Project Consultant: Kathryn Copsey

ACKNOWLEDGMENT

With thanks to Moira Kleissner, a member of the CURBS Resource Team, whose contributions have further enriched the thinking and activities set out in Colours of Easter.

Contents

Foreword

This is an *exciting* book. We re-live the events at the heart of the Christian faith. The story engages with us, both children and adults—with our feelings, our own experiences, as well as our minds. We are exposed to something of the violence and pain as Jesus dies, as well as the breathtaking joy of the resurrection.

It is also a *practical* book. Liz and Christine write from real experience and understanding of urban children and their surroundings. The resources they suggest are easily obtained, and not too demanding financially. The suggestions start leaders off in a way that helps to make sure that children's ideas are listened to, and that they are used to shape what happens.

It is a *responsible* book. There is help on everything from Child Protection to electrical safety, with guidelines to keep children safe as, with adults, they leave the security of well-tried methods and approach the Easter story in new ways.

And it is a book that *works*! On an urban estate one year, a whole primary school was involved, with each class taking a colour. Another time, I co-ordinated the very different groups that used it, including an after-school club and a school Christian club as well as a church Sunday group, who all came together for a memorable final presentation.

I thoroughly recommend *Colours of Easter* as both inspiring and down to earth. Adults will learn with and from children as the Easter story comes to life.

Over the last ten years, CURBS has produced resources that have worked in a variety of urban contexts. In a non-church club, the material allowed children to be real about problems they faced. Currently, I am using their materials as a source of ideas for Sunday worship. And I have encouraged others—teachers, club leaders and Sunday group leaders—to use the material in different ways too. I hope you will join them.

Revd Sue Allen, Church of the Resurrection, Grovehill, Hemel Hempstead

About CURBS

CURBS stands for 'Children in URBan Situations'. It is a charity that aims to provide resources, training and support for children's workers in inner cities and on outer urban estates, particularly those who are working with children from non-book, non-church backgrounds.

WHAT IS THE STARTING POINT FOR CURBS?

Children in urban situations need to make sense of their streetwise, confused and often hurtful world. The core values that underlie CURBS are about building relationships, building self-worth and enabling children to meet Jesus. CURBS is about coming alongside a child and 'being' Jesus for him or her. It is about taking time: long-term commitment to the children, their families and their community.

CURBS has a threefold aim:

* To produce low-cost resources which start in the child's world, value the child's innate spirituality and do not assume any Bible knowledge.
* To provide ongoing support and training for children's workers based in urban areas.
* To network with groups and individuals who have an understanding of the spiritual and developmental needs of children in urban communities and who are also working to support such communities.

FROM THE GROUND UP

A key aspect of CURBS is our concern to be responsive to the needs and experiences of those working on the ground. We don't want to be just another attractive resource: we want to 'scratch where it itches'! Our Resource and Training Teams came together out of a common concern about the lack of resources and training to meet the needs of urban children. We are all practitioners. We haven't got all the answers but we hope that we are heading in the right direction. We welcome your ideas and input.

STREETS AHEAD!

The vision for CURBS originated in East London in the 1970s. This vision finally became a reality in 1999 when CURBS was set up as a registered charity. Over the years, we have established a firm base of interest, prayer and support. Our resources are used throughout the United Kingdom and overseas. We train small and large groups. If you are interested in finding out more, we'd love to hear from you. Contact us at info@curbsproject.org.uk or visit our website at www.curbsproject.org.uk.

PART ONE

Preparation

Introduction

WHAT IS *COLOURS OF EASTER* ALL ABOUT?

Using the ideas in this book, you can help children aged 5 to 10 (and adults, if you choose) to present the story of Jesus' trial, death and resurrection. The material is designed to help you learn more deeply about the experiences that Jesus went through in the last week of his life and the significance of those events for our life today. The aim is to help you relate your own experiences to those of Jesus, to appreciate more of the joy of the resurrection—and discover more about God's love for you.

The presentation is in seven sessions—an introduction and six other sessions, each using a colour (or colours).

Session 1: Introduction to the project, methods of presentation and the Bible story (Matthew 12:1–14; 23:1–7, 23–28; 26:1–5)

Session 2: Blue: Jesus is betrayed and arrested (Luke 22:39–48, 52–53)

Session 3: Purple: Jesus is accused, mocked and beaten (Mark 15:3–5, 15–20)

Session 4: Red: Jesus is crucified (John 19:16b–18, 28–30)

Session 5: Black: The death of Jesus (Luke 23:44–46, 48, 50, 52–53)

Session 6: White and yellow: The resurrection of Jesus (Matthew 28:1–3, 5–7a, 8–10)

Session 7: Green: Easter morning in the garden (John 20:11–18)

There is more information about each session in the 'Overview' chapter (pp. 13–14).

Hundreds of years before the invention of the printing press, when most people could not read, stained-glass windows were known as 'the poor man's Bible'. Together with colours, symbols, light, sounds and music, they were used to tell the stories of God's love for his world, so that everyone who went to the church could see, hear and understand. As you read through this material, you will see that visual and aural images are used to tell the Easter story. In non-book, multi-ethnic, urban communities where the storytelling tradition still flourishes in many forms, learning is by hearing, by seeing, by experiencing, by doing. This is the approach taken in the book.

HOW TO USE THE MATERIAL

The ideas in this book can be used in a number of different ways according to the time available and your situation. There are no right or wrong ways of using it. Here are a few basic ideas.

As an all-age presentation

Involve the children in preparing and presenting the story at an all-age service or special event. For example, Sessions 1–5 could be presented at a Good Friday service, with Sessions 6–7 presented on Easter Sunday; or perhaps you might like to present the whole story on Easter Sunday or another event arranged over the Easter weekend.

As a basis for a holiday club

Sessions 1–5 could be used during the week before Easter, perhaps on Monday to Friday, with Sessions 6–7 presented on Easter Sunday; or why not use it all at other times of the year? Each session includes outline suggestions for related activities.

For groups that meet weekly

The seven sessions could form a Lenten project, with the group working on one session each week leading up to a presentation over the Easter weekend.

For small groups

With a few children, work on one session at a time and choose methods of presentation that need less people: for example, using an overhead projector and shadow images. The same children can present each session without changes of costume.

For large groups

With large numbers, split the children into groups to prepare one session per group. You will probably need at least two adults to each group (especially if the groups are working in different rooms). The groups can work on their own sessions from the beginning to the stage of presentation. It will be important to have one person co-ordinating the sessions, keeping in touch with each group and working out how to fit the presentation together.

For younger children

If you have younger children (less than eight years old), try to enlist other adults or older children to assist, especially when asking questions after the Bible story has been told. You will also need plenty of help with any craft work and to support the children when deciding how to present the story. When giving choices, offer only two or three.

For mixed-age groups

With a mixed-age group, you could assign the younger children to Sessions 6 and 7 (and possibly Session 2) and give them extra adult support; or you could allow them to work alongside older children. Encourage them to contribute to the discussions, but provide alternative activities if they become restless. The alternative activities could be craft work using the colour of the session the group is working on, or other activities suggested in Sessions 2–7.

It is suggested that you encourage children to discuss and interact with the material rather than deciding yourself how to do the presentation beforehand. This will involve the children in the story and its meaning, and draw a deeper response from them. (If you are not familiar with this approach, please read the 'Essential information' chapter on pages 15–17. This gives tips for brainstorming and discussion.) Involving the children in this way may feel risky to you, but the results will make the risk worthwhile as you will be calling on the children's own creativity and developing their own ideas and insights into the Bible narrative.

WHAT IS INVOLVED IN THE PRESENTATION?

This book is intended to help you make a presentation of the Easter story with a group of children (or children and adults) who will be involved in deciding how to present and arrange it. There are several ways to present the story, all using Bible material and music (recorded or live) and/or sound effects. You might choose the same method of presentation for each session or use a variety of approaches. Whatever you choose, colour will be an important factor. The methods of presentation suggested in this book are:

- Using an overhead projector
- Shadow images with props and actors behind a screen
- Mime with actors wearing masks
- Freeze frame or tableau
- Actors wearing face paints

These approaches are explored in more detail in the 'Presentation methods' chapter (pp. 19–39).

WHERE DO WE BEGIN?

There are two main stages: preparation and presentation.

Preparation

First of all, explore the story by:

- wondering about it
- understanding it
- feeling it
- asking questions about it
- identifying with it

Next, decide how to present each session by:

- getting a feel for what is possible
- discussing how to help the audience have a meaningful experience
- trying out ideas
- planning and making props
- planning scripts

Then get everything ready by:

- rehearsing visuals and sound
- inviting friends, family and community
- checking that everyone knows what they are doing
- preparing the room, arranging refreshments and so on

Presentation

The presentation consists of the story of Jesus' trial, death and resurrection, using:

- light
- colour
- images
- sound
- music
- Bible reading or a script that follows the Bible narrative closely

The best ideas will be those that come from the children when you explain the idea and explore the Bible passages together. Please don't take the ideas in this book as the ones you must follow. They worked very well in one situation—on an estate in Hull—but they may not suit your situation. You may have better ideas or extra ideas.

AND FINALLY...

The aim of this book is to set you thinking, not to give you all the answers. Suggestions for the presentation are outlined in the 'Presentation methods' chapter (pp. 19–39).

The presentation may only last for 20 minutes. If you are holding a special event, include refreshments and time to chat to make it a real occasion. Perhaps games could be provided for smaller children after the presentation.

You can use sounds and/or music to accompany the visual presentation. The type of music is suggested in the 'Overview' chapter (on page 13) and in each session. Examples are given, but you could easily use your own ideas or present the children with options. Some children may only know a narrow range of music, so it's a good idea to introduce them to other types.

You may find it helpful to ask other people for suggestions, such as others in your church, a local primary school music co-ordinator, the church music group or organist. A visit to the CD section of your local library may also help. Take a copy of the 'Overview' chapter with you to remind you what you are looking for.

Overview

SESSION 1

* Colour: None needed
* Introduction
* Theme/emotion: Danger, tension
* Sound/music: Music that creates tension, for example:
  - 'The Approaching Menace' (theme tune from *Mastermind*)
  - 'Dance of the Knights' from *Romeo and Juliet*, Prokofiev
* Bible base: Matthew 12:1–14; 23:1–7, 23–28; 26:1–5

This session is an essential introduction to the whole project. It is suggested that, whatever format you have chosen, this will be the first session for everyone. The introduction covers:

* why Jesus was in danger of arrest and death
* the Jewish rulers' jealousy because of his popularity with the crowds
* their anger because they thought he was breaking important rules
* how Jesus challenged the rulers
* Jesus' refusal to deny claims that he was the Messiah (the person expected to bring God's rule on earth)

SESSION 2

* Colour: Blue
* Theme/emotion: Betrayal, sadness
* Sound/music: Soft, melancholy music, for example:
  - Slow movement from *String Quintet*, Schubert
  - 'Lacrimosa', *Requiem for My Friend*, Preisner
  - *Song for Athene*, John Tavener (used at Princess Diana's funeral)
* Bible base: Luke 22:39–48, 52–53 (Jesus is betrayed and arrested)

SESSION 3

* Colour: Purple
* Theme/emotion: Violence, fear
* Sound/music: Mocking laughter/discordant music, for example:
  - 'Dance of the Knights' from *Romeo and Juliet*, Prokofiev
  - 'Mars' from *The Planet Suite*, Holst
  - Overture to *Romeo and Juliet*, Tchaikovsky
* Bible base: Mark 15:3–5, 15–20 (Jesus is accused, mocked and beaten)

SESSION 4

* Colour: Red
* Theme/emotion: Pain, terror
* Sound/music: Hammering, harsh music, for example:
  - Opening of *Organ Concerto*, Poulenc
  - *Gloria*, Poulenc
* Bible base: John 19:16b–18, 28–30 (Jesus is crucified)

SESSION 5

* Colour: Black
* Theme/emotion: Death, grief
* Sound/music: Silence or music full of raw emotion, for example:
  - *Adagio for Strings*, Barber
  - 'Nimrod', from *Enigma Variations*, Elgar
  - *Variations on a Theme of Thomas Tallis*, Vaughan Williams
  - Slow movement from *String Quintet*, Schubert
  - 'Lacrimosa', *Requiem for My Friend (Part 1)*, Preisner
  - *Song for Athene*, John Tavener (used at Princess Diana's funeral)
* Bible base: Luke 23:44–46, 48, 52–54 (The death of Jesus)

SESSION 6

- ✲ Colour: White/yellow
- ✲ Theme/emotion: Resurrection, amazement
- ✲ Sound/music: Percussion; energetic, joyful music, for example:
  - Opening of *Also Sprach Zarathustra*, Richard Strauss (used in *2001: A Space Odyssey*).
  - Central section of 'Jupiter' from *The Planet Suite*, Holst
  - Instrumental 'Sunrise' section of *The Creation*, Haydn
  - 'Morning' from *Peer Gynt*, Grieg
  - *Ave Verum Corpus*, Mozart
- ✲ Bible base: Matthew 28:1–3, 5–7a, 8–10 (The resurrection of Jesus)

SESSION 7

- ✲ Colour: Green
- ✲ Theme/emotion: Celebration, joy
- ✲ Sound/music: Energetic, joyful music, for example:
  - *Russian Easter Festival: Overture*, Rimsky-Korsakov
  - 'La Réjouissance' from *Music for the Royal Fireworks*, Handel
  - 'Et Resurrexit' from *B minor Mass*, J.S. Bach
  - 'Autumn Bacchanal' from the ballet *The Seasons*, Glazounov
- ✲ Bible base: John 20:11–18 (Jesus meets his friend in the garden)

Essential information

BRAINSTORMING AND DISCUSSION TECHNIQUES

When preparing to brainstorm, make sure you are clear about the task that you want the group to perform. In your use of *Colours of Easter*, the task may be to explore the feelings that were aroused during the telling of the Easter story, or it may be to explore the group's own experiences and emotions connected with the story. Another time, it may be to come up with ideas for a practical project: for example, how to present the story of Jesus' betrayal in the garden.

Have large sheets of paper and pens ready to jot down ideas, words or phrases that arise, but don't hold up the flow of the discussion unnecessarily to write things down. If you find it hard to write quickly or while people are still talking, give the job to someone else or recap what has been said at the end. Your primary aim is to get people talking freely about the task in hand. Don't let anything get in the way of that.

Gathering the group

Make sure that everyone can see you and each other. About eight children is a good number for a discussion. If you have more, it may be difficult for the quieter children to speak with confidence. Make sure that everyone knows what the aim of the discussion is. Say, for example, 'We are going to think about the story we've just heard. I'm wondering what you thought about it.'

Asking questions

Always try to ask questions to which there could be a variety of answers. These are called open questions. They invite thought and honest answers. 'Wondering' questions are a good example: 'I wonder whether you've ever felt like that...?'; 'I wonder what might have happened next...?' 'How' and 'why' questions are good too: 'How shall we do this?' or 'Why do you think this might work?'

Closed questions, by contrast, invite a limited range of answers and are more likely to give the impression that you are looking for 'right' answers from the children, rather than wanting them to think for themselves. 'Did Jesus feel sad?' for instance, invites only 'yes' or 'no'. 'How did Jesus feel?' invites the children to use their imagination and insight. The children are also free to add to the answers given by others: 'Sadie said he might have been sad, but I think he was glad too because he was doing what God wanted.'

You should aim to let your group know that you value their ideas, their thoughts and their feelings, but you needn't feel that you have to comment on everything that is said. A smile, a nod and word of thanks for the contribution will let the speaker know that you've heard and accepted what has been said.

Listening

For some group leaders, just listening is very difficult! It can feel scary to allow the pauses and digressions that are part of a natural discussion. Of course, if the silence or the digression is too long, you need to move things on, but don't exercise control too readily. If you do, you'll miss the whole point, which is helping the children to think, feel, react and plan. You'll end up with only your own ideas. These ideas may be brilliant, of course! However, the children will not really own them in the way that they will if the thoughts are really their own.

Drawing things together

You will notice that the group's interest begins to wane after a while. (As they grow more confident in you as a leader and more used to this way of working, their attention span will increase.) Begin to draw the discussion to a close as soon as you see that the children are no longer concentrating very well. You can summarize what has been said very briefly if you wish, especially if there was any disagreement, so that both sides can see that you've heard them.

In conclusion, thank everyone for taking part and lead on to the next part of the programme.

CHILD PROTECTION AND 'DISCLOSURE'

Children's welfare is at the heart of all we do. It's important, therefore, that we comply with the law intended to protect them from harm. While we regret that such measures are necessary, we can be glad that the welfare of children is taken so seriously nowadays. Everything suggested here is intended to ensure that our children are treated well and are, as far as possible, in no danger while they are with us. This means that we have to be careful about who is engaged to work with children and how we treat the children.

Many denominations have Child Protection Guidelines based on the Home Office document, *Safe from Harm*. Check that your church has a copy either of the denominational guidelines or the Home Office document and is adhering to it. If you are unsure, ask your church leader, who should at least tell you how to get in touch with your denominational office. If your church is non-denominational and has no policy on child protection, contact the Home Office for a copy of their guidelines. The Churches' Child Protection Advisory Service will answer questions and can provide training in working with children as well as setting up a policy and the correct systems within your church. Their address is Churches' Child Protection Advisory Service, PO Box 133, Swanley, Kent, BR8 7UQ. Telephone: 01322 667207; e-mail: info@ccpas.co.uk or visit www.ccpas.co.uk.

People working with children should hold a CRB (Criminal Records Bureau) enhanced level certificate of disclosure. This is a legal requirement and is not optional. The Criminal Records Bureau contact address is PO Box 110, Liverpool L3 6ZZ. The application telephone number is 0870 90 90 344. The disclosure website is www.disclosure.gov.uk. Your church should have a 'Child Protection Policy' and be able to help you with applications for disclosure.

Please make sure that the following actions are taken for your children's work. The whole church is responsible, and it should not be left to the children's workers themselves.

- As already stated, people working with children should hold a CRB (Criminal Records Bureau) enhanced level certificate of disclosure. This is a legal requirement and is not optional.
- There should be a 'named person' in your church who can deal with any queries and who has received training on this issue.
- There should have been some training for people working with children in your church. This can be done through your 'named person', denomination, CCPAS, NSPCC or your local authority.
- There should be a policy on, or understanding of practice about, what is appropriate when touching or disciplining children.
- There should be a recognized system for dealing with disclosures (that is, where a child talks about being ill-treated or bullied at home, at school or in another location by friends, family or strangers). Children's workers should on no account take it on themselves to tackle these problems or to go to the child's parents. They must be dealt with through the correct channels or immeasurable harm can be done to the child. Although disclosures are very rare indeed, we must be prepared correctly.

All this may sound labour-intensive, but in actual fact it is not as onerous as it appears. We do have to conform to the present law and be seen to have models of good practice in place. This will not only protect our children, and protect those who work with them from false accusation, but will be a good witness to our community.

Colours of Easter touches very sensitive issues concerning hurt, betrayal, abuse and death. Our aim is not to upset children or create problems, but it may be that a child will find an opportunity through learning about the Easter story to speak about something hurtful that has never been discussed before. If this is the case, it is important to be prepared, know how to deal with it and how to take care of the child. Let's make sure that we honour Christ by adhering to good practice, no matter what inconvenience it may cost us personally.

USING PARENTS AS HELPERS

Where possible, use parents to help with your sessions. It is a great idea to get parents involved with the children, so that they not only discover what the children are learning about but also gain a different perspective on what they themselves know and believe. Most people think only about mums, grandmas, aunts and female friends when working with children. Don't forget to involve fathers, older brothers, grandads and uncles. Many children need good male role models, so include both sexes when seeking helpers. If men don't volunteer, go and ask them to help. They may never have considered working with children, but they have much to offer.

There are some ground rules that need establishing before you include parental help. These should be sorted out before the adults actually start working with the children.

- *All* adults working with children need CRB clearance (see above).
- Make sure that the adults helping know who is leading the sessions. Some helpful and over-enthusiastic parents can take over, with the best intentions in the world. Be clear on what they are expected to do before you start.
- Run though your strategies for dealing with disruptive children from the beginning. It is usually better to ask parents to leave the leaders to deal with any problems. Otherwise, parents may try to interfere (with the best intentions) and not realize that they are causing conflict. If parents are unhappy about a situation, any discussions should take place after the session, not during it.
- Rather than having parents standing around, give them specific jobs to do, such as cutting things out, sharpening pencils, mounting artwork, tidying up and so on. They may not see what needs doing unless you draw it to their attention, or they may feel unhappy about doing something you haven't asked them to do.
- Use parents who have musical ability to play instruments or lead singing, if you include music in your sessions.
- Sometimes parents will chat at the back of the room throughout a session. Don't allow this to happen. Not only is it rude to the leaders, but it also distracts the children. Before you start, ask parents politely not to have conversations while leaders are doing activities (if it is an emergency, they should have the conversation outside the room). Mobile phones should be turned off.
- A parent who is a teacher may seem an obvious choice as a helper or co-leader. However, don't presume that they will want to help or be part of the team. They may wish to spend their free time in other ways. On the other hand, they may be very willing and may bring useful insights, techniques and strategies that are second nature to them. Be willing to learn new methods from them. The maxim is: ask, don't presume, and certainly don't put them under any pressure. They have enough of that during the week at school.
- If you are dividing parents up among groups of children, it is always wise to not have them in the same group as their own child. It may seem cruel but it usually stops children demanding their parent's individual attention, and prevents accusations of favouritism or even of ignoring their own child completely.

Parents are great to work with. When they are involved, it gives the message that children are important in the family of God and are not something to be pushed away into the corner. Jesus reprimanded his disciples for sending the children away. Let him be our example in giving time to children and their families.

LINKS WITH SCHOOL EXPERIENCE

In schools today, children discuss, think and learn about a wide variety of topics in Personal, Social and Health Education. There are many ways in which PSHE overlaps with Religious Education in general and Christianity in particular. For instance, children will be engaged in exploring aspects of emotions, friendship, bullying and the world around them. All these areas are developed within *Colours of Easter*. The children will find resonances between many of the questions raised here and what they are learning at school.

Much is talked about spirituality in the curriculum and ethos of the school. This involves asking questions, discussing and wondering about life, friends, and the world around, and feeling a sense of awe and wonder about what we experience. These themes are embedded within the teaching, discussion and activities of *Colours of Easter*.

By making use of discussion, by allowing the children to listen to each other and giving them space to express what they feel and experience, we can help them make links between PSHE in school and what they are doing in their church-based groups.

HEALTH AND SAFETY

If you are working with a mixed-age group, ensure safety at all times. Keep control of running games so that younger children are not knocked over or trodden on by older children. When using scissors, always use those designed for children, with blunt blades and plastic-coated handles.

Food allergies

In Sessions 2–7, you will find suggestions for snacks based on the appropriate colour. Please ensure that you are aware of any food allergies before giving the children food. Parental consent forms should be given to the children attending the sessions, with a section asking for information about food allergies included on the form.

PART TWO

Presentation Methods

This section gives a range of different methods that you can use to present the 'Colours of Easter' story. It is suggested that you choose one (or at most two), and present each session using your chosen method(s).

Using an overhead projector

The simplest method of presentation is to use an overhead projector. Colours and props are placed on top of the glass and projected on to a screen or blank wall. If you do not have an overhead projector, you may be able to borrow one from a local school or neighbouring church or college.

Colours can be produced by using coloured transparencies or the 'gels' used for theatre lights (a local theatre or amateur dramatic society may be able to lend them to you). Props can be laid on the projector deck to cast images on to the screen. Sometimes you can use the real thing: for example, a hammer and nails. At other times you will make something to represent the real object: for example, a whip made from string, or images made from card to produce a silhouette.

Here are some tips for using overhead projectors.

Make it clean

Overhead projectors are sometimes used for years, gathering dust and smears that spoil the image being projected. You will probably need to unscrew the top (with the power disconnected) to take the glass off and carefully clean it on both sides.

Make it large

Use the largest blank wall or screen that you can find. Experiment with moving the projector backwards and forwards to make the largest possible square of light on the wall.

Make it bright

Black out windows if possible or hold the presentation after dark. This will make it more effective and allow for fewer distractions.

Make it 'professional'

Get to know how the projector operates:

- how to focus the image
- how to place the image on the wall or screen
- how to move the image to the right place on the screen by using the mirror

Always have a spare bulb ready to switch to if needed.

Make it unusual

You may have used an overhead projector for a long time, but perhaps there are new ways to try. Experiment with the children, finding ways of projecting silhouettes, colours, patterns and shapes. Try using water in a glass dish and adding drops of food colouring (but be sure to keep the water in the container and cover the projector with plastic film to prevent any drops of liquid from contacting electrical parts).

Other ways of producing colour on the screen are by

colour photocopying a picture or background on to a transparency, or by using cellophane: for example, sweet wrappings.

Make it flow smoothly

Set the projector on a large table. Setting it on the floor is possible, but not safe if very small children are likely to be present. Establish a pattern so that everyone taking part knows that visuals are moved from right to left. Those that have been shown are placed on the left, and those that have not are ready in the correct order on the right. This avoids creating a muddle that might spoil the presentation.

Avoid the mistake of standing in the way of the screen! Experiment to find the best way of sitting or kneeling (or standing, for shorter people) as you operate the projector.

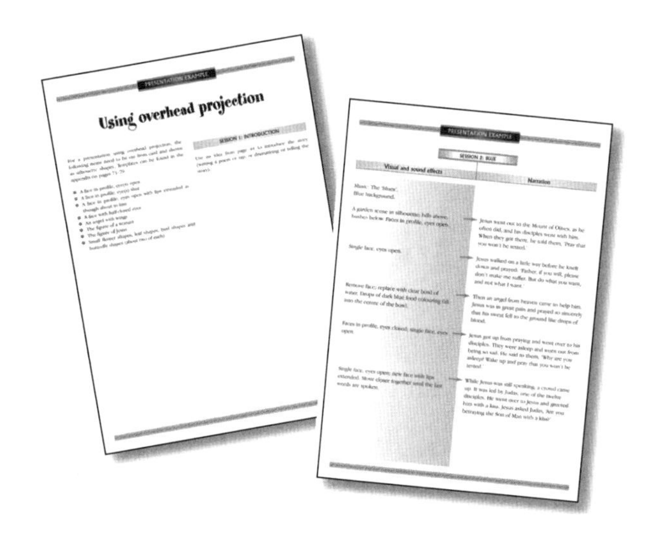
PRESENTATION EXAMPLE

Using overhead projection

Visual and sound effects

Narration

An activity to introduce children to the use of an overhead projector can be found on page 43. For an example of presentation using overhead projection, see pages 22–28.

Using overhead projection

For a presentation using overhead projection, the following items need to be cut from card and shown as silhouette shapes. Templates can be found in the appendix on pages 71–79.

* Faces in profile, eye(s) open
* Faces in profile, eye(s) closed
* A face in profile, eyes open with lips extended as though about to kiss
* A face with half-closed eyes
* An angel with wings
* The figure of a woman
* The figure of Jesus
* Small flower shapes, leaf shapes, bird shapes and butterfly shapes (about two of each)

SESSION 1: INTRODUCTION

Use an idea from page 44 to introduce the story (writing a poem or rap, or dramatizing or telling the story).

SESSION 2: BLUE

Visual and sound effects	Narration
Music: The 'blues'. Blue background.	
Faces in profile, eyes open.	Jesus went out to the Mount of Olives, as he often did, and his disciples went with him. When they got there, he told them, 'Pray that you won't be tested.'
Single face, eye open.	Jesus walked on a little way before he knelt down and prayed: 'Father, if you will, please don't make me suffer. But do what you want, and not what I want.'
Remove face; replace with clear bowl of water. Drops of dark blue food colouring fall into the centre of the bowl.	Then an angel from heaven came to help him. Jesus was in great pain and prayed so sincerely that his sweat fell to the ground like drops of blood.
Faces in profile, eyes closed; single face, eye open.	Jesus got up from praying and went over to his disciples. They were asleep and worn out from being so sad. He said to them, 'Why are you asleep? Wake up and pray that you won't be tested.'
Single face, eye open; new face with lips extended. Move closer together until the last words are spoken.	While Jesus was still speaking, a crowd came up. It was led by Judas, one of the twelve disciples. He went over to Jesus and greeted him with a kiss. Jesus asked Judas, 'Are you betraying the Son of Man with a kiss?'

SESSION 3: PURPLE

Visual and sound effects	Narration
Taunting, cruel laughter. Purple background.	
Two silhouette faces.	The chief priests brought many charges against Jesus. Then Pilate questioned him: 'Don't you have anything to say? Don't you hear what crimes they say you have done?' But Jesus did not answer, and Pilate was amazed.
Outline of hands; whip made by binding lengths of string together.	Pilate ordered his soldiers to beat Jesus with a whip and nail him to a cross.
Face with half-closed eye.	The soldiers led Jesus inside the courtyard of the fortress and called together the rest of the troops.
Fine-meshed fabric or netting draped across the glass; twisted branches for crown of thorns; ruler on the glass.	They put a purple robe on him, and on his head they placed a crown that they had made out of thorn branches. They made fun of Jesus and shouted, 'Hey, you king of the Jews!' Then they beat him on the head with a stick. They spat on him and knelt down and pretended to worship him. When the soldiers had finished making fun of Jesus, they took off the purple robe. They put his own clothes back on him and led him to be nailed to a cross.
Voices and music fade.	

PRESENTATION EXAMPLE

SESSION 4: RED

Visual and sound effects	Narration
Sad music. Red background.	
Loop of rope on glass; rulers crossed.	Jesus was taken away and he carried his cross to a place known as 'The Skull' in Aramaic; this place is known as 'Golgotha'.
Wood on wood sound; nails and hammer.	There Jesus was nailed to the cross, and on each side of him a man was also nailed to a cross.
Bowl of water with red food colouring.	Jesus knew that he had now finished his work. And he said, 'I am thirsty!' A jar of cheap wine was there. Someone then soaked a sponge with the wine and held it up to Jesus' mouth. After Jesus drank the wine, he said, 'Everything is done!'
Sounds stop.	

SESSION 5: BLACK

Visual and sound effects	Narration
Silence. OHP light shining on to screen.	
'Eclipse': light almost blotted out by large plate or cover.	Around noon, the sky turned dark and stayed that way until the middle of the afternoon. The sun stopped shining, and the curtain in the temple split down the middle.
Total darkness.	Jesus shouted, 'Father, I put myself into your hands!' Then he died.
Weeping.	A crowd had gathered to see the terrible sight. Then, after they had seen it, they felt broken-hearted and went home.
Soft, sad music.	There was a man named Joseph who was from Arimathea in Judea. Joseph went to Pilate and asked for Jesus' body.
Stone rolled against stone; silence for up to a minute.	He took the body down from the cross and wrapped it in fine cloth. Then he put it in a tomb that had been cut out of solid rock and had never been used.

SESSION 6: WHITE AND YELLOW

Visual and sound effects	Narration
Energetic music, quiet at first, gradually getting louder.	
Cloth across glass, letting through minimum light.	The Sabbath was over, and it was almost daybreak on Sunday when two women named Mary went to see the tomb. Suddenly a strong earthquake struck and the Lord's angel came
Rumble, percussion crash; stone rolled against stone.	down from heaven. He rolled the stone away and sat on it.
Cloth pulled away, revealing the outline of a stone at the side of the screen and an angel silhouette with wings made of feathers at the centre.	The angel looked as bright as lightning, and his clothes were as white as snow. The angel said to the women, 'Don't be afraid! I know you are looking for Jesus, who was nailed to a cross. He isn't here! God has raised him to life, just as Jesus said he would. Come, see the place where his body was lying. Now hurry! Tell his disciples that he has been raised to life.'
	The women were frightened, and yet very happy, as they hurried from the tomb and ran to tell the disciples.
Cover screen with collage made of yellow cellophane (for example, sweet wrappings).	

PRESENTATION EXAMPLE

SESSION 7: GREEN

Visual and sound effects	Narration
Bird song. Green background.	
Figure of a woman at one side of the glass.	Mary Magdalene stood crying outside the tomb.
Figure of Jesus added, a little apart.	She turned around and saw Jesus standing there, but she did not know who he was. Jesus asked her, 'Why are you crying? Who are you looking for?' She thought he was the gardener and said, 'Sir, if you have taken his body away, please tell me, so I can go and get him.'
Add flowers, leaves, birds, butterflies in silhouette; move figures closer together.	Then Jesus said to her, 'Mary!' She turned and said to him, 'Teacher!'

Using shadow images

Shadow play is a traditional form of theatre and may suit your situation, especially if there is a dais or stage on which to perform. Experimentation is just as important for this method.

Here are some tips for using shadow images.

Make it large

Use a large white sheet stretched from the floor to its full height and from left to right. Shine a bright light behind the sheet and project shadows on to the sheet from behind. You will need to experiment with this to see how best to make the shadows of people and props in the most effective way. The props will be much larger than those used for OHP, in most cases in scale with the actors.

Make it bright

Use coloured lights (a local theatre or drama group may be able to lend you these), ideally rigged with a proper control box. If this is too ambitious, use a series of lights of different colours, switching from one to another as the presentation proceeds.

Make it 'professional'

Careful rehearsal is a must, so that everyone knows exactly what to do next and where the props are for each part. Practice will show you how the actors need to pose to make each gesture and how the props need to be held to give the best image. Ideally, teach several people to present each part so that it doesn't matter if some don't turn up at the last moment. Try to persuade everyone behind the scenes to keep quiet throughout the presentation to avoid distracting the audience.

Make it unusual

Try not to settle for the safe options when choosing how to present the story. There will be much more satisfaction in taking a few risks to make a really memorable performance. Use recorded or live music, and link the sessions with percussion instruments: for example, drums using the same rhythm each time.

Make it flow smoothly

Rehearse thoroughly right from the beginning, not only the individual sessions, but the changes from one to another. Everyone should know where he or she needs to be next and which props are needed. This may be very hard to achieve at first, but the children will grow in self-esteem as they see the quality of what they are presenting.

An activity to introduce children to the use of shadow images can be found on page 43. For an example of presentation using shadow images, see pages 33–39.

Using freeze frame

A 'freeze frame' is a group of actors together creating an event that is frozen in time, rather like a still photograph. This is an effective way of helping the children to 'get inside' an event or story.

Here are some tips for using freeze frame.

Make it well planned

Begin with some warm-up activities to help the children 'get inside' the situation and the characters. Read the relevant Bible passage aloud. Discuss the events, the situations and the characters. What is happening in the story? Who are the main characters? How do you think they are feeling? Who is talking to whom? What is the most important part of this part of the story? The children may well have different ideas.

Make it well rehearsed

The idea of freezing an event or action may be a new idea to the group, although children may well have learned similar techniques in their dance or drama classes. ('Musical statues' is a good game to introduce this approach.) Begin by inviting the children to use their bodies to pantomime different activities suggested in the passage. In Session 2, you could explore actions such as sleeping or praying. How might you sit or lie if you are sleeping... if you are praying... if you are in distress? What body language, gestures and facial expressions might you use? Once the children have experimented with different ideas, invite them to choose one position and 'freeze' in that position for 30 seconds.

Make it co-operative

Now get the group to choose one particular event or part of the story in each session to dramatize. (In the 'Ideas for presentation' on pp. 33–39, a scene is suggested, but if you choose to present the Easter story using only tableaux, you may like to give the group the option to illustrate aspects of the story of their choice.) Let them choose together which characters they are going to play. Some of the group can become props as well. For example, in Session 2, some children can be trees on the Mount of Olives; one could be a rock that the sleeping disciples lean against; Judas might appear from behind another child who is posing as a bush.

Make it 'professional'

Now work on creating the tableau (or 'holding the freeze'). This will take plenty of practice as the children need to be very still. Use the example of a still photograph to help the children grasp the idea. You could take photos of the different tableaux when they are finalized. This can be very affirming for the children, as it records the thought and effort that they have put into creating the scene. If you are presenting the scenes to a congregation or audience, choose one child to be the 'director'. His or her task is to identify the event or part of the story represented and to point out the different characters and describe what they are doing.

Once the children have prepared and practised the scenes, and before any final presentation, you may like to spend some time exploring with them how it felt to be a part of the various tableaux. Was it hard to be still—to be 'frozen'? How did it feel to be able to communicate an emotion or an action—to tell a story—without saying a word?

Make it effective

Ideally, if you are presenting the story to an audience as a series of freeze frames, you will need a curtain to hide each change of scene. Alternatively, use a sheet, lengths of material or wallpaper, or dim the lights. Between each scene change, have someone read the relevant Bible passage, accompanied by appropriate music. The music can continue to play for 30 seconds or so as the audience looks at the scene and before the 'director' gives his or her explanation.

An activity to introduce children to the use of freeze frame can be found on page 43. For an example of presentation using freeze frame, see pages 33–39.

Using face paints

If you choose to use face paints, the actors will need to develop mime or dance actions to accompany the script. They should also dress in the same colour as their faces are painted. The face painting, the script and the costumes will all have to be considered by the group.

Make it effective

The best way to apply blocks of colour is to use sponges and not brushes. Face paints can be easily applied on anyone, old or young, but to get the best effect use a range of shades of the same colour blended over the face, rather than just one flat colour. For example, light blue could be used round the outside of the face, blending into gradually darker blue shades and eventually a purple over the nose and central face. The rule is to start with light either on the outside, as described above, or in the centre, and place close shades next. If you put light blue next to purple, you will lose the essential blueness. The same is true of every colour used.

Make it safe

The following rules should be always followed, on health and safety grounds. We have a duty of care for those we work with in churches, so we need to exercise caution. Always get permission from parents (preferably written) before face painting. You will then be covered in the case of a totally unexpected reaction that may require a doctor or hospital treatment. A simple form with a signature and date will suffice. Always use recognized hypo-allergenic CE-registered face paints. Never use unlabelled paints: you won't know if they are safe. If the paints are more than two years old, take care and test the product on your own face first.

Teach the children who will be applying the paint to observe the following safety rules:

- Always make sure that the paints are clean. Wipe with fresh water and a clean cloth for each person.
- Always wash out sponges and brushes in clean water between people, and use clean water for each face.
- Never paint children under three years old (their skin can react violently, even with hypo-allergenic paints).
- Never paint anyone with cuts, sores, spots, cold sores or eczema. Face paints can irritate the condition and can also spread infection.
- Ask everyone to wash his or her face first. Check that the face is thoroughly clean (no food around the mouth, for instance). A tub of baby-wipes is an extremely useful resource.

Make it 'professional'

Take the time and trouble to get the very best results that you can. This means plenty of practice and experimentation. Be sure to get the right paints for the best effect:

- Never use ordinary make-up or stage make-up, but always water-based paint from a recognized company.
- Don't use stage blood: parents won't thank you when they can't get the stains out of clothes.
- The best paints to use are 'Snazaroo', which can be bought in many shops. However, for the full range of colours and shades, get their catalogue. They also stock sponges, brushes and safety notes. Contact them by telephone on 01643 707659 or try their website: www.facepaintshop.co.uk. 'Snazaroo' are very quick on delivery and helpful on the phone.

Make it flow smoothly

As each session is worked on, some thought should be given to continuity—how to move easily from one session to the other. This may be done with music, percussion instruments or changes of lighting. Rehearse the links as thoroughly as the sessions for an effective performance.

An activity to introduce children to the use of face paints can be found on page 43. For an example of presentation using face paints, see pages 33–39.

Using masks

As with face paints, if you choose to use masks, the actors will need to develop mime or dance actions to accompany the script. They should also dress in the same colour as their masks are painted. The masks, the script and the costumes will all have to be considered by the group.

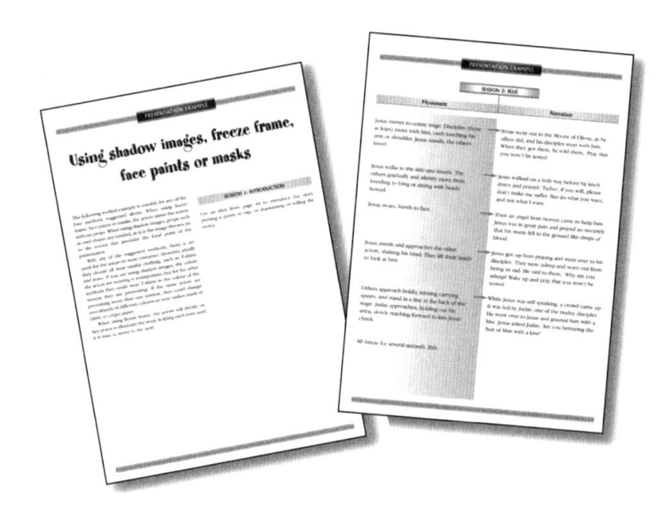
PRESENTATION EXAMPLE

Using shadow images, freeze frame, face paints or masks

Make it effective

The best way to make simple masks is to use card for a masquerade-style eye mask on a cane. A template can be found on page 80 of the Appendix. Cut the masks out of stiff card and attach a short cane, such as a garden cane, to one side using clear sticky tape or masking tape. Alternatively, make a hole at either side of the mask and use shirring elastic to attach the mask around the head.

Colour the masks according to the colour of the session, using as many different shades of that colour as possible, where appropriate. The children could dress in T-shirts of the same colour. The children simply hold the mask up to their face as they mime the script.

Make it safe

Ensure that the children are responsible with the masks. If using canes, discourage the children from using the cane for horseplay or to jab other children. With younger children, an elastic fastening is the safest option.

Make it 'professional'

Take the time and trouble to get the very best results that you can. This means plenty of practice and experimentation. Be sure to get the right paints, such as acrylics or poster paint, for the best effect. With older children, you could experiment with spray paint, but this must be done out of doors, with close adult supervision and plenty of newspaper to protect surfaces.

Make it flow smoothly

As each session is worked on, some thought should be given to continuity—how to move easily from one session to the other. This may be done with music, percussion instruments or changes of lighting. Rehearse the links as thoroughly as the sessions for an effective performance.

For an example of presentation using masks, see pages 33–39.

Using shadow images, freeze frame, face paints or masks

The following worked example is suitable for any of the four methods suggested above. When using freeze frame, face paints or masks, the actors mime the action without props. When using shadow images, props such as card shapes are needed, as it is the image thrown on to the screen that provides the focal point of the presentation.

With any of the suggested methods, there is no need for the actors to wear costumes. However, ideally they should all wear similar clothing, such as T-shirts and jeans. If you are using shadow images, the colour the actors are wearing is unimportant, but for the other methods they could wear T-shirts in the colour of the session they are presenting. If the same actors are presenting more than one session, they could change into tabards of different colours or wear sashes made of fabric or crêpe paper.

When using freeze frame, the actors will decide on key poses to illustrate the story, holding each pose until it is time to move to the next.

SESSION 1: INTRODUCTION

Use an idea from page 44 to introduce the story (writing a poem or rap, or dramatizing or telling the story).

SESSION 2: BLUE

Movement	Narration
Jesus moves to centre stage. Disciples (three at least) move with him, each touching his arm or shoulder. Jesus stands, the others kneel.	Jesus went out to the Mount of Olives, as he often did, and his disciples went with him. When they got there, he told them, 'Pray that you won't be tested.'
Jesus walks to the side and kneels. The others gradually and silently move from kneeling to lying or sitting with heads bowed.	Jesus walked on a little way before he knelt down and prayed: 'Father, if you will, please don't make me suffer. But do what you want, and not what I want.'
Jesus sways, hands to face.	Then an angel from heaven came to help him. Jesus was in great pain and prayed so sincerely that his sweat fell to the ground like drops of blood.
Jesus stands and approaches the other actors, shaking his head. They lift their heads to look at him.	Jesus got up from praying and went over to his disciples. They were asleep and worn out from being so sad. He said to them, 'Why are you asleep? Wake up and pray that you won't be tested.'
Others approach boldly, miming carrying spears, and stand in a line at the back of the stage. Judas approaches, holding out his arms, slowly reaching forward to kiss Jesus' cheek.	While Jesus was still speaking, a crowd came up. It was led by Judas, one of the twelve disciples. He went over to Jesus and greeted him with a kiss. Jesus asked Judas, 'Are you betraying the Son of Man with a kiss?'
All freeze for several seconds. Exit.	

SESSION 3: PURPLE

Movement	Narration
(The same group of actors can mime all actions, excluding Pilate's and Jesus'.)	
Jesus stands centre stage; the others around him, arms folded.	The chief priests brought many charges against Jesus.
Pilate walks around Jesus, wagging finger. Jesus stands still.	Then Pilate questioned him: 'Don't you have anything to say? Don't you hear what crimes they say you have done?' But Jesus did not answer, and Pilate was amazed.
Pilate pushes Jesus towards the others. They take hold of him and walk him around the stage.	Pilate ordered his soldiers to beat Jesus with a whip and nail him to a cross. The soldiers led Jesus inside the courtyard of the fortress and called together the rest of the troops.
With Jesus at the centre, the actors mime the actions in the narration. Jesus stands still.	They put a purple robe on him, and on his head they placed a crown that they had made out of thorn branches. They made fun of Jesus and shouted, 'Hey, you king of the Jews!' Then they beat him on the head with a stick. They spat on him and knelt down and pretended to worship him. When the soldiers had finished making fun of Jesus, they took off the purple robe. They put his own clothes back on him and led him to be nailed to a cross.
They all take hold of Jesus and freeze. Exit.	

SESSION 4: RED

Movement	Narration
Very slowly, Jesus walks, as though carrying a cross. Others walk behind and in front.	Jesus was taken away, and he carried his cross to a place known as 'The Skull' in Aramaic; this place is known as 'Golgotha'.
Two actors take Jesus' arms and stretch them wide. Two others stand on either side in the same pose. (Long pause.)	There Jesus was nailed to the cross, and on each side of him a man was also nailed to a cross.
Jesus lifts head as though speaking. An actor mimes giving him the wine on a sponge. All other actors step back.	Jesus knew that he had now finished his work, and he said, 'I am thirsty!' A jar of cheap wine was there. Someone then soaked a sponge with the wine and held it up to Jesus' mouth.
All other actors kneel, looking at Jesus. Freeze.	After Jesus drank the wine, he said, 'Everything is done!'

SESSION 5: BLACK

All actors except Jesus kneeling, heads bowed. Begin with one light focused on Jesus standing with arms outstretched, head bowed. Turn light off; two actors drape Jesus' body in black.	Around noon, the sky turned dark and stayed that way until the middle of the afternoon. The sun stopped shining, and the curtain in the temple split down the middle.
All remain still.	Jesus shouted, 'Father, I put myself into your hands!' Then he died.
All actors except Joseph and Jesus stand in pairs or threes, and exit, stumbling, holding each other up.	A crowd had gathered to see the terrible sight. Then, after they had seen it, they felt broken-hearted and went home.
Joseph stands looking at Jesus.	There was a man named Joseph, who was from Arimathea in Judea. Joseph went to Pilate and asked for Jesus' body.
Joseph takes the body of Jesus, still draped in black, in his arms and places him gently on the floor, looks at him for several seconds and then leaves.	He took the body down from the cross and wrapped it in fine cloth. Then he put it in a tomb that had been cut out of solid rock and had never been used.
Silence for up to a minute.	

PRESENTATION EXAMPLE

SESSION 6: WHITE AND YELLOW

Movement	Narration
Still dark, the two Marys walk slowly to centre stage.	The Sabbath was over, and it was almost daybreak on Sunday when two women named Mary went to see the tomb.
Lights on, focused on angel dressed simply in white.	Suddenly a strong earthquake struck and the Lord's angel came down from heaven. He rolled the stone away and sat on it.
The two Marys stand looking at the angel as he dances around them, inviting them to look centre stage, which is empty.	The angel looked as bright as lightning, and his clothes were white as snow. The angel said to the women, 'Don't be afraid! I know you are looking for Jesus, who was nailed to a cross. He isn't here! God has raised him to life, just as Jesus said he would. Come, see the place where his body was lying.
Pause after this line. The two women look where the angel is pointing and their attitude changes to excitement and joy.	
	'Now hurry! Tell his disciples that he has been raised to life.' The women were frightened, and yet very happy, as they hurried from the tomb and ran to tell the disciples.
The women exit.	

SESSION 7: GREEN

Movement	Narration
Mary stands looking down at the place where Jesus' body has been.	Mary Magdalene stood crying outside the tomb.
Jesus approaches and stands behind her. She turns, with head still bowed. Jesus looks at her, smiling, but she still weeps and looks down.	She turned around and saw Jesus standing there, but she did not know who he was. Jesus asked her, 'Why are you crying? Who are you looking for?' She thought he was the gardener and said, 'Sir, if you have taken his body away, please tell me, so I can go and get him.'
Pause after the word 'Mary'. She looks up, amazed, and kneels at his feet. They freeze.	Then Jesus said to her, 'Mary!' She turned and said to him, 'Teacher!'
All those taking part enter dressed in green, carrying flowers, confetti and streamers, and perform a joyful dance.	

PART THREE

Presentation

Introduction

This session introduces:

- the idea of the presentation
- some of the possible methods of presentation
- the way in which colours can be associated with emotions

Theme/emotion

Danger, tension

Sound/music

Music that creates tension, for example:

- 'The Approaching Menace' (Theme tune from *Mastermind*)
- 'Dance of the Knights' from *Romeo and Juliet*, Prokofiev

A large selection of Frank Zappa's music fits this mood.

Bible base

Matthew 12:1–14; 23:1–7, 23–28; 26:1–5

BIBLE NOTES FOR LEADERS

This part of the presentation sets the scene for the other six sessions. It tells the audience about the events that led up to Jesus' arrest and explains why he was in such danger. Everyone taking part in the presentation should be familiar with the story, which is told later in this session.

As we read the story, we see that Jesus didn't avoid confrontation, but neither was he looking for trouble. He readily challenged the hypocrisy of the religious authorities who were meant to be role models for others. He knew that their mistaken attitudes were actually preventing people from coming to God. They were encouraging people to focus on ritual actions, including a multitude of restrictions involved in keeping the Sabbath, instead of following the scriptures by behaving justly, with mercy and humble obedience to God (see Micah 6:6–8).

Jesus' message fell largely on deaf ears, for the religious leaders were too entrenched in their ways. Furthermore, they chose to use their power to destroy Jesus. They had to be careful, though, because Jesus was very popular with the ordinary people, who responded to his love and care. That is why they rarely tried to confront him in public and why they plotted secretly to engineer an end to Jesus that was both quick and efficient.

WARM-UP ACTIVITIES

Choose from the activities below, according to the methods you wish to use for the presentation. You could choose several, including 'Colours', ask the children afterwards which one or two they enjoyed most, and then focus on those for the other sessions. Alternatively, you could choose 'Colours' and one or two others that you feel confident about. The aim of the warm-up activities is to allow the children to experience using the methods to help them come up with ideas for the presentation of the Easter story.

Colours

You will need:
- paint colour charts

Provide some paint colour charts and ask the children to imagine that they can paint their rooms in their favourite colours. Try to find out why they like particular colours and dislike others. Develop this idea by asking what associations different colours have: for example, red for danger, green for jealousy, white for cleanliness and so on. The children should think of their own ideas.

To develop the activity further, provide paper and coloured pens, paints or chalks. Invite the children to produce abstract designs using colours to represent different emotions.

Light

You will need:

- ✣ an overhead projector
- ✣ a screen or plain wall on which to project transparencies
- ✣ coloured OHP pens (non-permanent, if possible)
- ✣ cellophane paper (for example, sweet wrappings)
- ✣ loosely woven cloth
- ✣ cardboard
- ✣ scissors

Show the children how to use the equipment safely and what sort of image can be produced using the pens, cellophane, cloth and shaped cardboard. Form small groups of children (about two or three) and ask each group to produce a picture or abstract design that expresses something about themselves—their characters, their interests, their activities and so on. When these have been completed and shown, talk together generally about how the best images are produced.

Shadow images

You will need:

- ✣ a large white sheet
- ✣ a light source to place behind the sheet to make a 'shadow screen'

Experiment by trying different body shapes behind the shadow screen. Then form small groups of three or four children and give each one an emotion to portray: for example, sorrow, anger, jealousy, joy, delight, satisfaction. With younger children, work out first what the emotion means by giving them examples of what might have happened to produce each emotion. Working together, each group should try to portray the emotion they've been given through their movements and the shapes they produce on the shadow screen. Discuss how to produce the most effective images on the shadow screen.

Freeze frame

You will need:

- ✣ a camera

Choose a well-known story, perhaps a fairy story such as 'The Three Little Pigs'. Ask the group to think how they might tell this story through photographs. Suggest a number of photographs, perhaps just six to eight. The children should plan the poses they will need, using no props (or very few).

When the photographs have been taken, discuss what has been learnt through doing this activity. Explain that using the 'freeze frame' technique, they can illustrate a story by choosing key moments. They freeze the action in the first pose they have chosen while the story is read, move to another pose at the right moment, and so on.

Face paints

You will need:

- ✣ face paints in different colours (please read page 31, which explains precautions to be taken when using face paints)

Explain briefly how to apply the paints and suggest that everyone should experiment with them by applying them to their own hand. The children could produce a face or an abstract design, or just experiment with colour. Introduce the idea of using different colours to illustrate the different stages of a story for a performance.

EXPLAIN THE PROJECT

At this point in the session, you should explain to everyone that you are going to stage a presentation of the Easter story using colour, music, movement, sound effects and so on. The purpose is to help each other and your audience (if you are having one) to understand more about what happened to Jesus in the last days of his life—and how he came alive again.

To put the arrest, trial and death of Jesus into context, tell the following story.

The story

Jesus was very popular. People crowded around him all the time and he always welcomed them. Everybody knew about Jesus—how he made people who were unwell better, how he helped people, how he talked about God in ways that everyone could understand, not using difficult words that other religious teachers used.

But that was the trouble: other religious teachers didn't like the way crowds rushed to listen to Jesus and ignored *them*. *They* couldn't heal anyone. *They* didn't want to help people who were hurt. And they liked using difficult words that showed how clever they were.

But, for the religious teachers and leaders, it was worse than that! Jesus broke the rules. There were hundreds of rules that people who belonged to the Jewish faith were supposed to keep—about how to wash your hands before eating, how far you were allowed to walk on the Sabbath (which was the Jewish day of rest), who you were allowed to mix with, and lots of other things. It made the religious teachers angry to see so many people listening to Jesus. He talked about God, not about the rules.

But it was even worse than that! Jesus began telling off the religious teachers and leaders. He told them they were so blind that they couldn't see how wrong they were. They were always showing off about how good they were, saying long prayers in the streets and boasting about how well they kept the rules, but really they were worse than anyone else.

The worst thing of all was that some people were saying that Jesus was sent from God. The religious teachers and leaders hated hearing that. They thought, 'How can a man sent from God not follow the rules?' They met together and decided to get rid of him. All they needed was a chance to arrest him without the crowds around him.

Questions to ask

Ask some of the following questions (you needn't ask them all). Aim to make the story real by getting the group to identify with it.

About the Bible story

- How did the religious teachers and leaders feel when they saw how popular Jesus was?
- What might Jesus' friends have felt when they saw that he had made enemies of the religious teachers and leaders? What might they want to do?
- Why do you think Jesus didn't run away when he realized that his enemies wanted to kill him?

About our own experience

- What might happen today that would be like the crowds following Jesus and ignoring the people they'd respected before?
- Has this ever happened to you or someone you know? What happened?
- How do you feel when you see or hear about people ganging up on others?

DECIDING HOW TO PRESENT THIS SESSION

Discuss with the children how they could create an introduction that would help people to understand why Jesus was in danger. They should use the thoughts and feelings that came out of the questions and answers.

Here are some ideas:

- Write a poem or rap.
- Tell the story using two or three voices.
- Dramatize the story, using one character to represent Jesus and dividing the rest of the actors into two groups: the crowd and the Jewish teachers and leaders. Keep the dialogue to a minimum. Ask two of the teachers and leaders to make comments about what is happening, while Jesus and the crowd mime a scene in which the crowd gathers excitedly and Jesus welcomes, teaches and shows concern for individuals.

Preparation

Once the method of presentation for the introduction has been decided, the children (or a small group) will need to work further on the session by:

- writing or improvising a poem or rap, or deciding how to use the Bible story
- experimenting with music and/or sound effects and lighting
- rehearsing
- making sure that the introduction is an attention-grabber

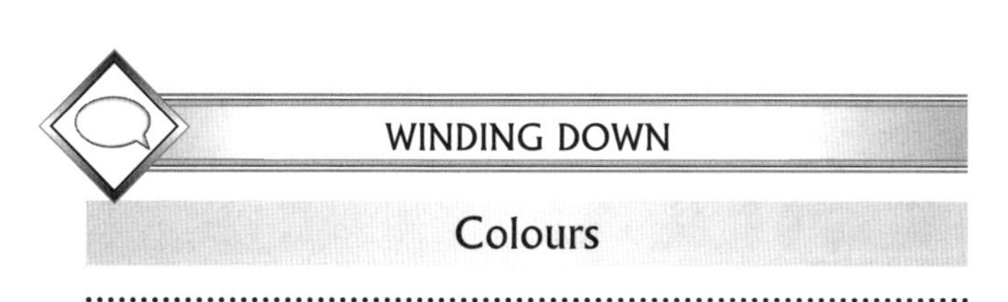

WINDING DOWN

Colours

You will need:

- a sheet of paper for each person
- coloured pens
- background music and a sound system

Scatter the pens around the room in places where it will be comfortable to sit and draw. Talk about the way in which colours are sometimes associated with our emotions. We might have more than one emotion at a time: for instance, be angry about one situation in our lives and happy about something else.

Give out the paper and ask the group to think about how they are feeling at present. They should go and find coloured pens that suit their emotions in some way, and draw or write with those colours to express how they feel. While they are doing this, they should be reminded that God understands both happiness and sadness.

Play background music during the activity.

Time to reflect

Draw everyone together and allow time for individuals to talk about how they felt about the activity.

Jesus is betrayed and arrested

COLOUR: BLUE

Theme/emotion

Betrayal, sadness

Sound/music

Soft, melancholic music, for example:

- Slow movement from *String Quintet*, Schubert
- 'Lacrimosa', *Requiem for My Friend (Part 1)*, Preisner
- 'Song for Athene', John Tavener (used at Princess Diana's funeral)

Bible base

Luke 22:39–48, 52–53

Jesus went out to the Mount of Olives, as he often did, and his disciples went with him. When they got there, he told them, 'Pray that you won't be tested.' Jesus walked on a little way before he knelt down and prayed, 'Father, if you will, please don't make me suffer... But do what you want, and not what I want.' Then an angel from heaven came to help him. Jesus was in great pain and prayed so sincerely that his sweat fell to the ground like drops of blood. Jesus got up from praying and went over to his disciples. They were asleep and worn out from being so sad. He said to them, 'Why are you asleep? Wake up and pray that you won't be tested.' While Jesus was still speaking, a crowd came up. It was led by Judas, one of the twelve apostles. He went over to Jesus and greeted him with a kiss. Jesus asked Judas, 'Are you betraying the Son of Man with a kiss?' ...

Jesus spoke to the chief priests, the temple police, and the leaders who had come to arrest him. He said, 'Why do you come out with swords and clubs and treat me like a criminal? I was with you every day in the temple, and you didn't arrest me. But this is your time, and darkness is in control.'

BIBLE NOTES FOR LEADERS

This story marks a moment of immense significance. Up to this point, Jesus was free to teach people about God. Afterwards, his fate was in the hands of those who were seeking to destroy him. Between these two points, Jesus prayed. He knew what was going to happen: if he took the path of obedience to God, he would have to be subject to the will of other people. Although every human instinct of survival and the desire to avoid pain was telling him to run away, he chose the difficult way—the way of humiliation, suffering and death.

However, although Jesus handed his *body* over to the authorities, he remained fully in control of his mind and his spirit. That strength of mind is available to us today from Jesus himself as we pray. Despite the sadness of this story, we see Jesus offering hope even in the darkest place.

WARM-UP ACTIVITIES

Thinking blue

You will need:
- a table
- a blue cloth
- blue items

Decorate the room using as many blue items as possible. Have an 'interest table' with a blue tablecloth and blue items that can be handled and talked about. Include as many shades of blue as possible. Talk about the colour—the associations it has, the mood it creates, what the children like and dislike about it.

Blue collage

You will need:
- a large piece of backing paper
- glue sticks or glue
- saucers and brushes
- scissors
- magazine pictures with blue areas

If you are working through all the sessions with the same group, plan and begin a large collage to continue over each session. For this session, blue could be part of a picture: for example, the sky in an Easter garden scene, or simply an abstract design (perhaps a circle with different coloured segments). Make it by tearing out or cutting and pasting blue snippets from magazine pictures.

If you have different groups working on each colour, you can use the same idea. In this case, have someone design the whole picture, cut it up into pieces and give the appropriate piece to each group.

WARM-UP GAMES

To link in with the story of Jesus in Gethsemane, play games around the theme of sleeping, not watching or not being ready. Here are some examples.

'Mr Bear, your honey's not there'

You will need:
- a blindfold
- a jar or other container

Blindfold a child, 'Mr Bear', who sits at the centre of a circle formed by everyone else. Next to the child, place some 'honey' (any kind of container). Mr Bear pretends to sleep while the others creep up, trying to grab the honey. If Mr Bear hears a noise, he opens his eyes and points at anyone still moving, who must then return to her place and start again. If someone manages to grab the honey, everyone can call out, 'Mr Bear, your honey's not there!'

Shipwreck

A series of commands are called out: for example, 'scrub the decks', 'salute the Captain', 'man the pump', 'climb the rigging'. The last person to mime the action is not ready and is called 'out'.

SNACK TIME

Have blueberry muffins and any blue drink you can find!

PREPARATION FOR PRESENTATION

Read Luke 22:39–48, 52–53 to the children, asking them to think about how Jesus felt and how his friends felt throughout the story. Alternatively, tell the story as follows.

Jesus is betrayed and arrested

It was dark as Jesus and his friends walked out into the street. It had been warm in the upper room where they'd eaten their special supper, but as they stepped into the cool night air, they wrapped their clothes around them. The friends walked without speaking, following Jesus. They knew that something was going to happen, something that

would change their lives. They felt sad and anxious. Jesus seemed sad too.

'Where's Judas?' someone whispered.

Nobody answered. They had seen him slip away during supper and they all knew that he was up to something—it was just that they weren't sure what. There were only eleven of them now.

They reached the garden without being noticed. They often came here. It was a good place to be quiet and to think. Jesus turned to them. 'Pray that you won't be tested,' he said. Then he went ahead of them. The friends could still see his dark shape as he dropped to his knees.

'He's praying,' they said to one another. 'Let's do the same.'

But they could hear Jesus' voice as he prayed: 'Father, if you will, please don't make me suffer. But do what you want, and not what I want.'

He sounded so terribly sad that they could hardly bear to listen. Their friend and leader was in such great pain that his sweat fell to the ground like drops of blood—and they could do nothing to help.

They listened for a while and then, one by one, worn out by their own terrible sadness, they fell asleep on the ground.

They woke up suddenly, not knowing how long they'd slept. Though it was dark, they could see Jesus standing looking at them. They rubbed their eyes, knowing that they'd let him down.

'Why are you asleep?' he asked. 'Wake up and pray that you won't be tested.'

But while Jesus was still speaking, a crowd came up. Some were carrying flaming torches, and the eleven friends could see quite clearly who was leading the crowd. It was Judas. He went over to Jesus and greeted him with a kiss. 'Jesus!' he said.

Jesus looked deeply into Judas' face. 'Are you betraying me with a kiss?' he asked.

Then he turned to the crowd that had come with Judas. They were religious leaders and their police, all armed with swords and clubs. Jesus had no protection. 'Why have you come to arrest me here,' he asked, 'when you could easily have done it any day in the temple?'

They had no answer.

'This is your time,' Jesus told them, 'and darkness is in control.'

They arrested him and took him away.

Questions to ask

Ask some of the following questions (you needn't ask them all). Aim to make the story real by getting the group to identify with it.

About the Bible story

- I wonder what you felt while you were listening to the story?
- What do you think Jesus' friends felt as they walked to the garden?
- What might Jesus have felt while he was praying?
- How do you think he felt when he saw that his friends were sleeping?

About our own experience

- I wonder if your friends ever let you down, or if you have ever let others down? What happened?
- What does the word 'betray' mean? Has this ever happened to you or someone you know? What happened? How did you feel?

Thinking about the colour

Talk about what you associate with the colour blue. Some of these ideas will be positive, some negative. List everything suggested. Discuss the way that blue is sometimes used to describe sadness. Introduce 'blues' as a style of music with downbeat, sad words. Play an example if possible.

DECIDING HOW TO PRESENT THIS SESSION

Make plans for presenting the Bible passage or the story to convey the emotions involved in betrayal and sadness. What sound effects or music will help the audience understand the story? What visual effects or props can be used?

If you choose to use overhead projection, see the example for 'Session 2: Blue' on page 23. For all other methods, see the example on page 34.

WINDING DOWN

You let me down!

Talk about times when people let their friends down. Choose one of the stories told as a result of this discussion, or create a fictional scenario and encourage the children to act or mime it.

Time to reflect

You will need

- a simple picture of a garden photocopied for each child (see page 70)
- pens

Provide each child with a simple picture of a garden, with flowers and trees in it. Ask them to draw or write something that makes them sad. If they wish, talk together about these things. Explain that Jesus was once very sad. He knows what it feels like and he can help us when we feel sad. Pray about sad things in general or, if the children wish, ask them to pray aloud about their own feelings of being sad.

Jesus is accused, mocked and beaten

COLOUR: PURPLE

Theme/emotion

Mockery, violence, fear

Sound/music

Mocking laughter/discordant music, for example:

- 'Dance of the Knights' from *Romeo and Juliet*, Prokofiev
- 'Mars' from *The Planet Suite*, Holst
- Overture to *Romeo and Juliet*, Tchaikovsky

A large selection of Frank Zappa's music fits this mood.

Bible base

Mark 15:3–5, 15–20

The chief priests brought many charges against Jesus. Then Pilate questioned him again, 'Don't you have anything to say? Don't you hear what crimes they say you have done?' But Jesus did not answer, and Pilate was amazed...

Pilate... ordered his soldiers to beat Jesus with a whip and nail him to a cross. The soldiers led Jesus inside the courtyard of the fortress and called together the rest of the troops. They put a purple robe on him, and on his head they placed a crown that they had made out of thorn branches. They made fun of Jesus and shouted, 'Hey, you king of the Jews!' Then they beat him on the head with a stick. They spat on him and knelt down and pretended to worship him. When the soldiers had finished making fun of Jesus, they took off the purple robe. They put his own clothes back on him and led him off to be nailed to a cross.

BIBLE NOTES FOR LEADERS

Jesus had been arrested by the Jewish authorities and now stood trial before the chief priests, the elders and the teachers of the Law. The odds were very much stacked against him. He was alone and this trial had been planned for a long time. They asked him to say whether he was the Messiah (the one sent by God who, they believed, would save the Jewish people from the Roman occupation of their land). They questioned him about being 'the Son of God'. Jesus claimed no status; he simply refused to answer, but that was enough to enrage the chief priests. The one thing they could not do was to condemn him to death. That is why they had to take him to the Roman governor, Pilate.

Before Pilate, the charges against Jesus changed completely. They knew that Pilate would not care whether or not Jesus claimed to be the Messiah or the Son of God. So they accused him instead of stirring the people up to rebel against the Roman emperor (Luke 23:1–2).

The Roman 'justice' system was brutal and efficient; we would regard what happened to Jesus as torture. It must have been terrifying, but the Gospel writers all agree about Jesus' composure through it all. Even Pilate was 'amazed' by him.

When we are in difficult situations of confrontation, we can be reassured by someone who understands how hard it can be. Jesus has been there too.

WARM-UP ACTIVITIES

Thinking purple

You will need:
- a table
- a purple cloth
- purple items

Decorate the room using purple, trying to find items for the interest table that reflect royalty, opulence and grandeur. Talk about the colour—the associations it has, the mood it creates, what the children like and dislike about it.

Purple collage

You will need:
- a large piece of backing paper
- glue sticks or glue
- saucers and brushes
- scissors
- magazine pictures with purple areas

If you are working through all the sessions with the same group, continue with the collage, using the colour purple. For example, you could use it for flowers or the clothes of a figure in an Easter garden scene, or add to your abstract design with torn or cut purple snippets from magazine pictures.

If you have different groups working on each colour, you can use the same idea. In this case, have someone design the whole picture, cut it up into pieces and give the appropriate piece to each group.

Group drama

Form older children into groups of four or five. Ask them to work together to create drama scenarios in which children are teased or bullied. Discuss how this might be done—thinking about how the action might begin, work to a climax and then end with some kind of resolution. Talk about ensuring that each group member will have a part to play. As they work, give guidance and help as needed. Allow about ten minutes for the groups to create their sketches and then ask the groups to act them one by one. Afterwards, talk about these situations together.

WARM-UP GAMES

To link in with the story of Jesus' unfair trial, play games that are clearly unfair and afterwards discuss with the children how it makes them feel when things are not fair.

Pick a slip

You will need:
- a box or bag
- slips of paper
- a list of challenges

Everybody should pick a slip of paper from a box. Two thirds of the slips are plain; the others have an 'x' marked on them. Only the children with an 'x' on their slip get the chance to do a challenge and get a prize (sweets, stickers, can of drink). The challenges could be standing on one leg for a minute, saying the alphabet backwards, singing a pop song without forgetting any words, making the group laugh or other simple tasks.

Purple wins

Play any game in which individuals can win or lose: for example, 'Simon says'. Afterwards, announce that only those wearing purple can win.

Carry the balloon

You will need:
- balloons (both large and small)

Form the children into teams of about five or six. Each team has four balloons. The first player must carry them to the end of the room and back again, give them to the next player, who does the same, and so on. If anyone drops a balloon, they must start again. The twist in this game is that one team will be given small balloons and the others will have large ones.

SNACK TIME

Have purple grapes and drink blackcurrant or summer fruits squash.

PREPARATION FOR PRESENTATION

Read Mark 15:3–5, 15–20 to the children, asking them to think about what was going on and why it was happening. Alternatively, tell the story as follows.

Jesus is accused, mocked and beaten

The high priest's house—that's where they took Jesus when he'd been arrested. It was barely light, but all the nation's leaders and religious teachers were there. It was their big chance to get rid of Jesus, and they were determined to make the most of it. They accused him of crimes he'd never committed and brought witnesses who lied about him.

Then they tied rope around his hands and took him to the Roman governor, Pilate, who had greater authority than they did.

Pilate asked Jesus, 'They accuse you of saying that you're the king of the Jews. Are you?'

Jesus didn't reply. He knew who he was and didn't need to prove it.

'Don't you have anything to say?' asked Pilate. 'Don't you hear what crimes they say you've done?'

Still Jesus didn't reply. Pilate couldn't believe that a prisoner would not try to defend himself, so he cruelly sent Jesus to be whipped and nailed to a cross. The soldiers took Jesus inside and made fun of him. They dressed him up in a purple robe, just like a king would wear; they made a crown out of thorn branches and pretended to greet him, shouting, 'Here is the king of the Jews!' They beat him on the head with a stick and then knelt down and pretended to worship him.

When they had finished making fun of Jesus, they put him back in his own clothes and took him outside and led him out to be crucified.

Questions to ask

Ask some of the following questions (you needn't ask them all). Aim to make the story real by getting the group to identify with it.

About the Bible story

- I wonder what your feelings were while you were listening to the story?
- What questions do you have about what happened?
- Who do you think is the strongest person in this story?

About our own experience

- Has anything unfair ever happened to you? How did you feel and what did you do?
- What makes people want to hurt others?
- What makes some people make fun of others?
- How does it feel to make fun of others?
- How does it feel to be the one who's being teased, mocked or bullied?

Thinking about the colour

Talk about what you associate with the colour purple. Purple, in Bible times, was to do with royalty or having power. Purple dye was very expensive, so only those who were rich and powerful could afford to wear purple clothes. Why was Jesus dressed in purple?

Purple is also the colour of bruises and can remind us of pain and violence.

DECIDING HOW TO PRESENT THIS SESSION

Make plans for presenting the Bible passage or story to convey the emotions involved in mockery, violence and fear. What sound effects or music will help the audience understand the story? What visual effects or props can be used?

If you choose to use overhead projection, see the example for 'Session 3: Purple' on page 24. For all other methods, see the example on page 35.

WINDING DOWN

Crowns

You will need:

- paper
- purple crayons
- pens or paints
- scissors
- sticky tape or a stapler

Younger children could make purple crowns as a symbol of royalty and wear them home.

Tie dye

You will need:

- white cotton T-shirts
- rubber bands
- purple multi-purpose dye
- saucepan with water
- salt

Older children could do this activity if there is time. Bunch a piece of the fabric in one hand and twist a rubber band tightly around it. Repeat this all over the T-shirt. Make the T-shirt completely wet and then mix the dye in the saucepan, add salt and put the garment in it, heating the saucepan, following the instructions on the packet. Remove the T-shirt and rinse it under the tap until the water is clear. Take off the rubber bands and dry the garment.

Time to reflect

Give out paper and purple crayons or pens. Invite the children to draw or write about something in the story of Jesus' trial and the way he was treated by the soldiers that they want to think about. Allow about five minutes and then pray this prayer.

Dear Jesus, we are sorry that you were treated unfairly and hurt. Help us to know that you are there with us when we are treated unfairly, or when we get hurt. Amen

Jesus is crucified

COLOUR: RED

Theme/emotion

Pain, terror

Sound/music

Hammering, harsh music, for example:

- Opening of *Organ Concerto*, Poulenc
- 'Gloria', Poulenc
- Various tracks by Nirvana
- Various tracks by Frank Zappa

Bible base

John 19:16b–18, 28–30a

Jesus was taken away, and he carried his cross to a place known as 'The Skull'. In Aramaic this place is called 'Golgotha'. There Jesus was nailed to the cross, and on each side of him a man was also nailed to a cross...

Jesus knew that he had now finished his work. And... he said, 'I am thirsty!' A jar of cheap wine was there. Someone then soaked a sponge with the wine and held it up to Jesus' mouth... After Jesus drank the wine, he said, 'Everything is done!'

BIBLE NOTES FOR LEADERS

Arrested and tried by the Jewish authorities, condemned to death by the Roman governor, Jesus was then sent to be executed under Roman law in one of the most horrific ways ever devised—crucifixion.

But the Gospel writers do not dwell on the horror of what happened to Jesus. They focus instead on the meaning of Jesus' suffering. God had sent him to earth with a purpose. He was to save humankind from sin, which had—for untold ages—prevented us from living as God intended. Jesus came to set us free to live in harmony with God.

When Jesus said, 'Everything is done!' it was a cry of triumph. In other versions of the Bible, the cry is, 'It is finished!' It is not a statement about the end of his life. It is much more than that. The way had been dark and hard, but Jesus had walked it without putting a foot wrong. Now he knew that everything God had sent him to do had been done.

Although this part of the story is the most horrific and the saddest, it contains the three words that bring hope and life to everyone who will accept them: 'Everything is done!'

How can we ever thank God enough for that?

WARM-UP ACTIVITIES

Thinking red

You will need:
- a table
- a red cloth
- red items

Decorate the room using as many red items as possible. Display items that convey warnings of danger or pain: for example, red-bordered road signs, traffic lights, warning lights, or Red Cross first aid items. Include as many shades of red as possible. Talk about the colour—the associations it has (danger, blood, fire, heat, love), the moods it creates, what the children like and dislike about it.

Red collage

You will need:
- a large piece of backing paper
- glue sticks or glue
- saucers and brushes
- scissors
- magazine pictures with red areas

If you are working through all the sessions with the same group, continue with the collage, using the colour red. For example, use red for a sunrise or the clothes of a figure in an Easter garden scene, or add to your abstract design with torn or cut red snippets from magazine pictures.

If you have different groups working on each colour, you can use the same idea. In this case, have someone design the whole picture, cut it up into pieces and give the appropriate piece to each group.

WARM UP GAMES

Play games to do with danger and trying to avoid getting caught. Here are some examples.

Islands

You will need:
- squares cut from cardboard boxes

Select one person to be the shark. The rest of the players have to stay out of the water (the floor space). Scatter the cardboard squares around the room. A player is only safe on an island (square of cardboard on the ground). They must move to another island when challenged by another player, and they are in danger of being caught by the shark while moving. When caught, they are eliminated. There are always fewer 'islands' than players.

Chase

Play other chasing games that the children know.

Board games

Play games such as Ludo or Snakes and Ladders, which present players with danger zones and safe places.

SNACK TIME

Have red jam sandwiches, strawberries, cherries or cherry tomatoes with raspberry squash.

PREPARATION FOR PRESENTATION

Read John 19:16b–18, 28–30 to the children, asking them to think about how Jesus felt and how other people felt. Alternatively, tell the story as follows.

Jesus is crucified

The sun was just getting hot when the Roman soldiers opened the gate of the fortress. The prisoner was not a brutal murderer, a mugger or a thief. He was Jesus, who had only ever done good things. Now he was doing the best thing of all.

The soldiers had given him a burden—the wooden cross on which he was to die. He carried it slowly and painfully through the streets until they came to a place called 'The Skull'. There Jesus was nailed to the cross, and on each side of him a man was also crucified.

The sun rose higher and sweat mixed with blood as the three men hung there.

Jesus knew what he was doing—dying for the wrong things others had done. And he knew that he had almost finished his work.

He called out, 'I am thirsty!'

Someone found a jar of cheap wine, soaked a sponge in it and held it up to Jesus' mouth. Jesus moistened his parched lips with the wine and then he took a last breath.

He cried out to the whole world, 'Everything is done!' He had completed the work that God had sent him to do.

Questions to ask

Ask some of the following questions (you needn't ask them all). Aim to make the story real by getting the group to identify with it.

About the Bible story

- I wonder what your feelings were while you were listening to the story?
- What was happening to Jesus in this story?
- Being nailed to a cross was a common thing to happen to criminals in those days. Why was it happening to Jesus?
- How would his friends and family be feeling at this time?

About our own experience

- What happens to us, or to people we hear about, that makes us feel the same way?
- What would you do or say if a friend was feeling sad and upset over something that had happened?

Thinking about the colour

Talk about the colour red and what is associated with it—perhaps blood, anger, love, embarrassment and danger. Where in the story might there be red things or feelings associated with red?

DECIDING HOW TO PRESENT THIS SESSION

Discuss how to convey the emotions of pain and terror behind the story. What visual aids and sound effects will make the words come alive? What kind of music would portray the emotions of the story?

If you choose to use overhead projection, see the example for 'Session 4: Red' on page 25. For all other methods, see the example on page 36.

WINDING DOWN

Suffering for faith

Explore stories of people who have suffered for their faith: for example:

- Oscar Romero. Useful material can be found at www.culham.ac.uk/cw/assemblies/001p_romero.php
- Cassie Bernall (Columbine High School). Visit the website, www.baptistfire.com/articles/ for information.

For further examples relevant to young people, see *Jesus Freaks* by dc Talk (Honor Books, 1999) or *Jesus Freaks Vol 2* by dc Talk (Kingsway Communications, 2002). Alternatively, visit www.jesusfreaks.com, or www.persecution.org. This site contains stories of people of all faiths and political stances persecuted for their beliefs, including current stories about Christians suffering for their faith.

Making crosses

For stained-glass crosses you will need:

- black paper or card
- coloured cellophane or tissue paper
- glue sticks or clear sticky tape
- scissors

Stained-glass window crosses can be made by cutting a cross shape out of black paper and pasting 'glass' on one side across the shape. The 'glass' could be coloured cellophane or tissue paper. Display on a window or near a light source.

Alternatively, simple wooden crosses can be created by binding twigs together with raffia, or model crosses can be made from Fimo, baking clay or dough.

With older children, research different kinds of crosses used as a Christian symbol. The book *A-cross the world* by Martyn Payne and Betty Pedley has the stories of over 40 crosses and a wealth of ideas for activities, crafts and games based on the cross (published by Barnabas, 2004).

Time to reflect

Use a simple hymn or song about Jesus' death, such as:

- It is a thing most wonderful
- There is a green hill
- Thank you for the cross

You could say or sing the words together and then discuss what the words say about why Jesus died. Close with a prayer of thanks to Jesus for dying for us.

The death of Jesus

COLOUR: BLACK

Theme/emotion

Death, grief

Sound/music

Silence, or music that explores grief, for example:

- *Adagio for Strings*, Barber
- 'Nimrod', from *Enigma Variations*, Elgar
- *Variations on a Theme of Thomas Tallis*, Vaughan Williams
- Slow movement from *String Quintet*, Schubert
- 'Lacrimosa', *Requiem for My Friend (Part 1)*, Preisner
- 'Song for Athene', John Tavener (used at Princess Diana's funeral)

Bible base

Luke 23:44–46, 48, 50, 52–53

Around midday the sky turned dark and stayed that way until the middle of the afternoon. The sun stopped shining, and the curtain in the temple split down the middle. Jesus shouted, 'Father, I put myself in your hands!' Then he died...

A crowd had gathered to see the terrible sight. Then after they had seen it, they felt brokenhearted and went home...

There was a man named Joseph, who was from Arimathea in Judea... Joseph went to Pilate and asked for Jesus' body. He took the body down from the cross and wrapped it in fine cloth. Then he put it in a tomb that had been cut out of solid rock and had never been used.

BIBLE NOTES FOR LEADERS

Three hours of darkness in the middle of the day might have been caused by an eclipse of the sun, but the natural cause is not the point of this story. It signified to those who watched the terrible thing that was happening, something that was shaking their whole world—the death of their friend and leader, God's beloved Son. Their hopes for a new future of peace and justice were ending. But the darkness was not the only 'sign' that day.

The curtain in the temple, referred to in the story, hid the Holy of Holies, the place that symbolized the very presence of God. Only one person ever passed through the curtain—the high priest—and only on one occasion each year—the Day of Atonement. It was as if, as Jesus died, the presence of God was thrown open to all. God was no longer secret and unknowable. Anyone can now have access to God.

The body of Jesus was treated with great respect by Joseph of Arimathea, but, despite his wealth and influence, burying it was all he could do. The next step was up to God.

WARM-UP ACTIVITIES

Thinking black

You will need:

- a table
- a black cloth
- night-lights (optional)

Illustrate this session's theme colour by bringing the children into a silent, darkened room. Have a leader outside to tell them what to expect and to ensure that they are ready. For younger children, have a night-light or small light shining to ensure that they are not frightened.

This time, don't have any items on the interest table—just a black cloth, to illustrate emptiness and death (absence of life). Talk about what you associate with the colour black. This might include funerals, formal clothes or Goths. (Be sure that there is no confusion between the expression 'black' in the sense of racial origin and black as the colour—or absence of colour.)

Black collage

You will need:
- a large piece of backing paper
- glue sticks or glue
- saucers and brushes
- scissors
- magazine pictures with black areas

If you are working through all the sessions with the same group, continue with the collage, using black. For example, use black for a border around the collage or the tomb in silhouette, or add to your abstract design with torn or cut black snippets from magazine pictures. Talk about how many shades of black there can be.

If you have different groups working on each colour, you can use the same idea. In this case, have someone design the whole picture, cut it up into pieces and give the appropriate piece to each group.

WARM-UP GAMES

Play games on the theme of rescue (to illustrate the point that Jesus' death was intended to rescue us).

Cross tag

One player is chosen as 'It' and tries to tag someone else. All other players must co-operate to prevent 'It' from tagging anyone. The game is lost if 'It' is successful. When 'It' is chasing someone, others can try to run between 'It' and the chased player to try to save him or her, but in doing so they put themselves in danger of being tagged. A tagged player becomes the next 'It'.

Rescue me!

Divide into teams of about four or five. Each team will be given a series of challenges, each one to be done by one team member at random. Write the challenges on pieces of paper and give one to each member of each team, so that all teams have the same challenges. Challenges could include: hop 50 times, do 20 sit-ups, stand on one foot for a minute, do 50 star jumps, run on the spot for two minutes.

Announce each challenge in turn and have the designated team member from each team step forward and begin on your command. Explain before they begin that if they wish to stop, they can shout 'Rescue me!' and the name of someone in their team, who will take over immediately. The winning team is the one to complete all the challenges first.

SNACK TIME

Have liquorice, blackcurrant muffins and a blackcurrant drink.

PREPARATION FOR PRESENTATION

Read Luke 23:44–46, 48, 50, 52–53 to the children, asking them to think about how Jesus felt and how other people felt throughout the story. Alternatively, tell the story as follows:

The death of Jesus

The sun was at its height, but there was no shade for the three men hanging on the crosses. Then, suddenly, the sky darkened! It was as though the sun had disappeared. It stayed that way until the middle of the afternoon.

In the temple, the great curtain that cut off from view the symbol of God's presence was torn in two from top to bottom.

Jesus gave a loud cry: 'Father, I put myself into your hands!' With that, he died.

Many of his friends were standing around, watching what was happening. When they saw that he was dead, they went home, broken-hearted, just as though something inside them had died too.

But one follower of Jesus, a man named Joseph who came from Arimathea, went to Pilate, the Roman governor, and said, 'The man Jesus is dead. Let me have his body.'

Pilate agreed, so Joseph had the body taken down from the cross. He wrapped it in the finest cloth and had it taken to a garden where there was an unused tomb, like a small cave built into the side of the rock. There he laid Jesus' body.

Questions to ask

Ask some of the following questions (you needn't ask them all). Aim to make the story real by getting the group to identify with it.

About the Bible story

- I wonder what your feelings were while you were listening to the story?
- What do you think Jesus meant when he said, 'Father, I put myself into your hands'?
- How might Jesus' close friends have felt about what happened to him?

About our own experience

- I wonder if you have ever felt that way when you heard that someone had died?
- What does it feel like to lose someone or something that you have loved?
- What helps us come to terms with losing someone or something we've loved?

Thinking about the colour

Talk about what emotions you associate with the colour black, such as sadness when someone dies, or feelings of hopelessness. Discuss the way that black is also absence of colour. What does it feel like to be in a dark place, such as an unlit room, or standing in the garden at night? Once again, be sure that there is no confusion between the expression 'black' in the sense of racial origin and black as the colour—or absence of colour.

DECIDING HOW TO PRESENT THIS SESSION

Discuss how to convey the emotions of death and grief behind the story. What visual aids and sound effects will make the words come alive? What kind of music would portray the emotions of the story?

If you choose to use overhead projection, see the example for 'Session 5: Black' on page 26. For all other methods, see the example on page 37.

WINDING DOWN

My story

You will need:

- a puppet (optional)

Tell a story (make it personal if possible) about someone close to you dying, perhaps using a puppet to talk through for younger children. Afterwards, invite the children to share their responses, either directly to you or talking to the puppet. Alternatively, they might like to make their own puppets to talk through. (It can be a lot safer to share feelings through a puppet.)

End on a positive note, saying that God helps us to come to terms with the death of someone we care about. We never forget them, but gradually we learn to remember all the good things we shared with the person who has died, as well as the sadness of losing them.

Time to reflect

Star and sun prayer

You will need:

- a box
- a star cut from tin foil or shiny paper
- a piece of black paper or fabric
- a yellow disc of paper almost covered in black (to represent a nearly eclipsed sun)
- a piece of fabric torn almost from top to bottom

Prepare a box with the items above to represent a star, dark sky, sun almost blotted out, and a torn curtain. Take the items out one by one, saying that when Jesus was born, a star travelled across the sky to show where he was. When Jesus died, the natural world went topsy-turvy: the sky turned dark, the sun stopped shining and the huge temple curtain split of its own accord. The Son of God, creator of the world, had died.

Encourage the group to think about Jesus from the appearance of the star at his birth, through his grown-up life, healing, teaching and helping, until his death on a cross. Ask everyone to think of something they'd like to say to Jesus, either silently or aloud. Close by reminding them that the death of Jesus is not the end. There's good news on the way!

The resurrection of Jesus

COLOUR: WHITE AND YELLOW

Theme/emotion

Resurrection, amazement

Sound/music

Percussion, energetic, joyful music, for example:

- The opening of *Also Sprach Zarathustra*, Richard Strauss (used in *2001: A Space Odyssey*)
- The central section of 'Jupiter' from *The Planet Suite*, Holst
- The instrumental 'Sunrise' section of *The Creation*, Haydn
- 'Morning' from *Peer Gynt*, Grieg
- *Ave Verum Corpus,* Mozart

Bible base

Matthew 28:1–3, 5–7a, 8–10

The Sabbath was over, and it was almost daybreak on Sunday when Mary Magdalene and the other Mary went to see the tomb. Suddenly a strong earthquake struck, and the Lord's angel came down from heaven. He rolled away the stone and sat on it. The angel looked as bright as lightning, and his clothes were white as snow…

The angel said to the women, 'Don't be afraid! I know you are looking for Jesus, who was nailed to a cross. He isn't here! God has raised him to life, just as Jesus said he would. Come, see the place where his body was lying. Now hurry! Tell his disciples that he has been raised to life…'

The women were frightened and yet very happy, as they hurried from the tomb and ran to tell his disciples. Suddenly Jesus met them and greeted them. They went near him, held on to his feet, and worshipped him. Then Jesus said, 'Don't be afraid! Tell my followers to go to Galilee. They will see me there.'

BIBLE NOTES FOR LEADERS

Jesus was definitely dead. He had been executed by professionals and his body carried to the tomb, which was sealed. There was no doubt in the minds of the two women returning to see the tomb. And so what they experienced was both strange and bewildering. A strong earthquake would have not been unknown, but was still unsettling. The appearance of a dazzling angel was presumably quite outside their experience.

At the time the women visited the tomb, Jesus was already risen from death. The removal of the stone by the angel was not to allow Jesus to leave the tomb, but for the benefit of the women, so that they could see that what they were told was true. It wasn't a fantasy induced by the shock of what had just happened. It was true: Jesus was no longer dead.

Their reaction of fright and joy has a ring of truth. How could they immediately take in what had happened? Although Jesus had predicted this very event, they had not understood it or taken it in. Matthew tells us that, suddenly, Jesus himself meets and greets them and gives clear instructions to go and tell his disciples—surely the most amazing news the world had ever heard!

WARM-UP ACTIVITIES

Thinking yellow and white

You will need:
- a table
- a yellow or white cloth
- yellow and white items

Decorate the room using as many yellow and/or white items as possible. Have an 'interest table' with a white and/or yellow tablecloth, displaying items that can be handled and talked about. If you choose yellow, include as many shades of yellow as possible. Talk about what you associate with the colours white and yellow. These might include cleanliness, sunshine, purity, brightness and hopefulness.

White and yellow collage

You will need:
- a large piece of backing paper
- glue sticks or glue
- saucers and brushes
- scissors
- magazine pictures with yellow and white areas

If you are working through all the sessions with the same group, continue with the collage, using yellow and white. For example, use these colours for the angel's wings, or a sunburst, or add to your abstract design with torn or cut white and yellow snippets from magazine pictures. Notice the contrast to the sombre colours of other sections.

If you have different groups working on each colour, you can use the same idea. In this case, have someone design the whole picture, cut it up into pieces and give the appropriate piece to each group.

WARM-UP GAMES

To link in with the story of Jesus' resurrection, play games around the theme of losing and finding, surprise, unusual outcomes.

Hunt my watch

Play a more sophisticated version of 'Hunt the Thimble'. While the seeker(s) is/are out of the room, three other players put personal items, such as a watch, badge, bracelet and shoelace around the room, but still visible. (If the group know each other well, the items could be given to and worn by other players.) The seekers have to find the objects and return them to their owners.

Open the box

You will need:
- a yellow or white sheet wrapped up as a 'pass the parcel'
- music and sound system

Say that you are going to play 'pass the parcel' with a difference. If you like, you can add some kind of treat between the layers. The person who opens each layer must say what they think might be in the centre, or what they hope will be there. Play in the normal way.

When the sheet is revealed at the end of the game, say that nobody guessed that there would be a sheet there! Explain that on the first Easter Sunday Jesus' friends expected to find Jesus' body in the tomb where it had been left. Instead they had a surprise: there was only the sheet in which his body had been wrapped.

SNACK TIME

Have bananas, egg slices or lemon buns, and lemonade to drink.

PREPARATION FOR PRESENTATION

Read to the children Matthew 28:1–3, 5–7a, 8–10, asking the group to imagine that they were friends of Jesus, going to the grave, expecting to find his dead body there. Alternatively, tell the story as follows:

The resurrection of Jesus

The sun was just beginning to peep over the horizon on Sunday morning when two women, both called Mary, set out from home. They were going to see the tomb where Jesus had been buried. It had all been so hasty on Friday after Jesus had died. They were sad as they walked together, thinking of the friend they had lost. As they entered the garden, they could see the tomb with a huge stone across the entrance.

Suddenly they were thrown to the ground by a strong earth tremor. When they looked up, they saw a dazzling angel, bright as lightning, rolling the stone away from the tomb, then sitting on it. They were terribly afraid and couldn't move.

The angel spoke gently: 'Don't be afraid. I know why you're here—to look for Jesus, who was nailed to a cross. But he isn't here! He's no longer dead, but alive! God has brought him back from death, just as Jesus said he would.'

The angel beckoned them forward. 'Come and see the place where his body was.'

The women stumbled forward and looked in the tomb. It was empty. They were astonished and full of awe.

The angel said, 'Go and tell Jesus' disciples what has happened. Jesus is alive! Hurry and tell them.'

The women turned and ran as fast as they could to tell the disciples. And then, suddenly, there was Jesus! He was standing in front of them, smiling, calling their names. The two women fell at his feet and worshipped him. He told them not to be afraid, but to hurry to the disciples. They had some amazing news to share.

Questions to ask

Ask some of the following questions (you needn't ask them all). Aim to make the story real by getting the group to identify with it.

About the Bible story

- I wonder what your feelings were while you were listening to the story?
- What good news did the two women hear?
- How might they have reacted to this news?

About our own experience

- What good news have you had lately?
- What news might make you feel the way the two women felt?
- How do people express happiness and amazement?

Thinking about the colour

Talk about the colours white and yellow and what is associated with each. For example, white is the colour of snow and is also the colour of light. What significance does white have in clothing? Yellow is the colour of sunshine and is associated with warmth and summer holidays on the beach. Discuss the way that yellow is used to describe happiness. Why have these two colours been put together for this part of the story?

DECIDING HOW TO PRESENT THIS SESSION

Discuss how to get a good transition from darkness and silence to the energetic mood of happiness and amazement. How might you convey the surprise of the news Jesus' friends heard?

If you choose to use overhead projection, see the example for 'Session 6: White and Yellow' on page 27. For all other methods, see the example on page 38.

WINDING DOWN

Resurrection energy

You will need:
- a sound system and recorded music or musical instruments

Using some energetic music, dance or do aerobics, which involve lots of energy and movement.

Good news

In small groups, discuss situations in which the children have received good news that made them happy (for example, passing an exam, hearing from a friend). Mime or act out some of the scenarios to the whole group. Together, talk about how we express our happy feelings (shouting, jumping, laughing and so on). How might you react to the news that Jesus is alive again? Play bright, hopeful music and allow the group to express resurrection joy in some of the ways suggested by the group.

Time to reflect

Stone painting

You will need:
- stones or pebbles
- paints and brushes
- varnish, glue and felt (optional)

Collect and wash some rounded stones or pebbles, suitable for painting. Use water-based paints and let the children paint something on an Easter theme—angel, sunburst, empty cross and so on. Use the finished stones as a focus for prayer.

If you wish, the stones could be varnished, with felt glued to the underside, to make paperweights to be given as an Easter gift.

Easter morning in the garden

COLOUR: GREEN

Theme/emotion

Celebration, joy

Sound/music

Energetic, joyful music, for example:

- *Russian Easter Festival: Overture*, Rimsky-Korsakov
- 'La Réjouissance' from *Music for the Royal Fireworks*, Handel
- 'Et Resurrexit' from *B minor Mass*, J.S. Bach
- 'Autumn Bacchanal' from the ballet *The Seasons*, Glazounov

Bible base

John 20:11–18

Mary Magdalene stood crying outside the tomb. She was still weeping, when she stooped down and saw two angels inside. They were dressed in white and were sitting where Jesus' body had been. One was at the head and the other was at the foot. The angels asked Mary, 'Why are you crying?' She answered, 'They have taken away my Lord's body! I don't know where they have put him.' As soon as Mary said this, she turned around and saw Jesus standing there. But she did not know who he was. Jesus asked her, 'Why are you crying? Who are you looking for?' She thought he was the gardener and said, 'Sir, if you have taken his body away, please tell me, so I can go and get him.' Then Jesus said to her, 'Mary!' She turned and said to him... 'Teacher'. Jesus told her, 'Don't hold on to me! I have not yet gone to the Father. But tell my disciples that I am going to the one who is my Father and my God, as well as your Father and your God.' Mary Magdalene then went and told the disciples that she had seen the Lord. She also told them what he had said to her.

BIBLE NOTES FOR LEADERS

All four Gospel writers agree that Mary Magdalene was present at the tomb on that Sunday morning, but only Matthew and John report that she met Jesus there. Here, in John's account, too full of tears to see clearly, Mary fails to recognize the risen Jesus. John tells us that this is her second visit to the tomb. She had first visited while it was still dark, and had run back to tell Peter and another disciple. She didn't say that Jesus had risen, but that someone had taken his body from the tomb and that she didn't know where they had taken him. This was so fixed in her mind that when she returned and met the angels, who asked her why she was crying, she simply repeated the bad news (v. 13). Then, when Jesus himself came to her, she repeated it again. It took one word only, spoken by Jesus, to change everything.

Her natural response was to cling to him. The words 'Don't hold on to me' could be translated as 'Don't go on holding on to me'. Jesus wanted her to go and tell others the good news, just as she had done when she'd thought the news was bad.

There may be variations of the story in the four Gospel accounts, but that doesn't detract from the central truth: Jesus is back from the dead and alive for ever. It's still the same good news that we share today!

WARM-UP ACTIVITIES

Thinking green

You will need:
- a table
- a green cloth
- green items, including plants

Decorate the room using as many green items as possible, including living plants if possible. Include lots of flowers and items that indicate new life. Pepper the room with green balloons and streamers. Have an 'interest table' with a green tablecloth, displaying green items that can be handled and talked about. Include as many shades of green as possible. Talk about the colour—the associations it has, the mood it creates, what the children like and dislike about it. These might include growing plants, jealousy, life, growth and so on.

Green collage

You will need:
- a large piece of backing paper
- glue sticks or glue
- saucers and brushes
- scissors
- magazine pictures with green areas

If you are working through all the sessions with the same group, finish the collage, using green. For example, use green for trees, plants or grass, or add to your abstract design with torn or cut green snippets from magazine pictures. Use different shades of green to get the effects of light and shade.

If you have different groups working on each colour, you can use the same idea. In this case, have someone design the whole picture, cut it up into pieces and give the appropriate piece to each group.

WARM-UP GAMES

To link in with the story of Jesus appearing after his resurrection, play games about recognizing people from clues given.

You'll never guess

Divide the children into two groups. Sit them with their backs to each other. Walk between the two lines and touch someone on the shoulder in one of the groups. That person should say (disguising their voice if they choose), 'You'll never guess who I am.' The other team has one guess as to who has spoken, and if they are right they gain a point for the team. If they are wrong, the other team wins the point. Continue, choosing someone from the other team to speak, and so on.

Self-portrait

You will need:
- paper and pens

Give each person a piece of paper and a pen. They should each draw themselves. Give a time limit for the drawing. Afterwards, display all the pictures on the wall or on a table. Everyone should try to guess who each drawing belongs to.

SNACK TIME

Have green apples, celery, cakes with green icing and lime squash.

PREPARATION FOR PRESENTATION

Read John 20:11–18 to the children, asking them to focus on how Mary begins to understand what has happened to Jesus. Alternatively, tell the story as follows:

Easter morning in the garden

It was very early, and the sun was still low in the sky, as Mary Magdalene stood in the garden that Sunday morning. There were signs of life all around her—the song of birds, flowers, trees and other plants growing silently in the earth—but Mary was thinking of only one thing: where was

the body of Jesus? It was terrible enough that he was dead, but who could have taken his body away? Why would anyone want to do that?

She bent down to look once again into the tomb and had the surprise of seeing, not an empty tomb as she'd expected, but two angels sitting where the body of Jesus had been, one where his head had been and one where his feet had been.

The angels asked Mary, 'Why are you crying?'

She answered, 'They have taken away my Lord's body! I don't know where they have put him.'

As soon as Mary said this, she turned around and saw Jesus standing there, but she didn't recognize him. She thought he must be the gardener.

Jesus asked her, 'Why are you crying? What are you looking for?'

She said, with tears in her eyes, 'If you have taken his body away, please tell me, so I can go and get him.'

Then Jesus said to her, 'Mary!'

It was only one word, but she recognized his voice immediately. She turned and said to him, 'Teacher!' She reached out to hold him, but Jesus told her, 'Don't hold on to me! I have not yet gone to the Father.'

With great joy, Mary Magdalene ran through the garden, now bathed in warm sunshine, through the streets to the room where his disciples were. 'I've seen the Lord!' she cried. 'He is alive! I've seen him with my own eyes.'

Questions to ask

Ask some of the following questions (you needn't ask them all). Aim to make the story real by getting the group to identify with it.

About the Bible story

- I wonder what your feelings were while you were listening to the story?
- Why do you think Mary was crying outside the tomb?
- What mistake did she make because of her sadness?
- How did she recognize Jesus at last?
- How might she have felt when she realized who he was?

About our own experience

- What might happen in life today to make you really happy?
- Are these things likely to finish quickly, or do they, like Mary's joy over Jesus being alive, change your life for ever?

Thinking about the colour

Talk about the colour green and what is associated with it, such as the foliage of trees, shrubs and plants, and emotions such as jealousy and envy. Where in the story might there be green things or feelings associated with green?

DECIDING HOW TO PRESENT THIS SESSION

Think of ways of using the colour green to give a feeling of celebration and joy. What visual ideas could be used to portray the joy in the story? What sounds or music will have the same effect? Work out how to bring the presentation to a conclusion (rather than just ending abruptly when the words finish). Perhaps an Easter hymn could be sung, with the words on decorated transparencies or photocopied paper.

If you choose to use overhead projection, see the example for 'Session 7: Green' on page 28. For all other methods, see the example on page 39.

WINDING DOWN

Easter banner

You will need:

- a large piece of green card or an old sheet
- collage materials
- a length of dowelling
- cord or string

Create an Easter banner showing the sun rising out of clouds and the words 'Jesus is alive!' You could use a large piece of green card or an old sheet as a background and use brightly coloured material or felt, gold cord, fabric pens and so on. Mount the banner on dowelling for hanging.

Easter song

You will need:
- ✤ paper and pens
- ✤ percussion instruments

Write a song together to celebrate Mary's discovery and her joy. Choose a simple, well-known tune, then write words to fit the rhythm (don't worry too much about making the lines rhyme). You could add percussion instruments. Alternatively, decide on a beat and write a rap.

Half face

You will need:
- ✤ photographs of well-known people or objects

Challenge the children to identify a well-known person or item from half a picture. Say that it is hard when you can only see partly. Mary didn't at first recognize Jesus or understand what she was seeing.

Time to reflect

Now that the collage picture is complete, sit the group in a circle and place the finished work in the centre. Use it to reflect on the story of Easter. Turn your reflections into prayer.

Appendix

Faces in profile, eye(s) open

Faces in profile, eye(s) closed

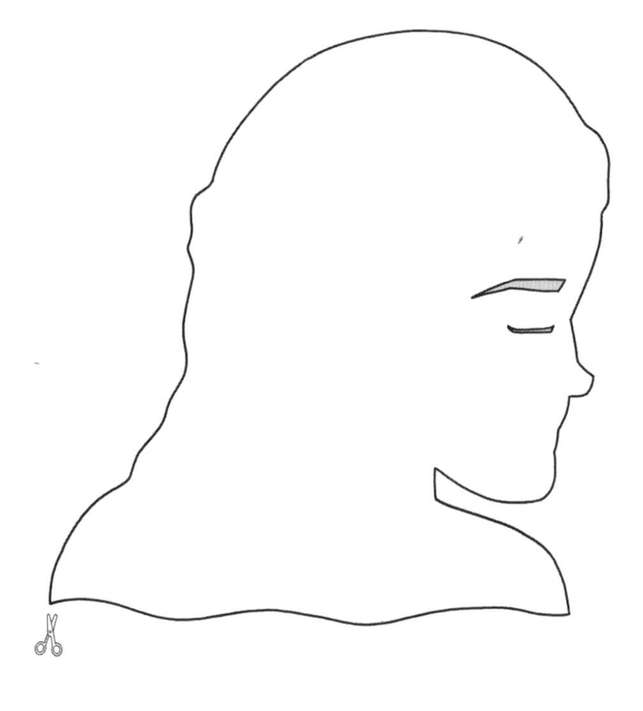

Face in profile, eyes open with lips extended as though about to kiss

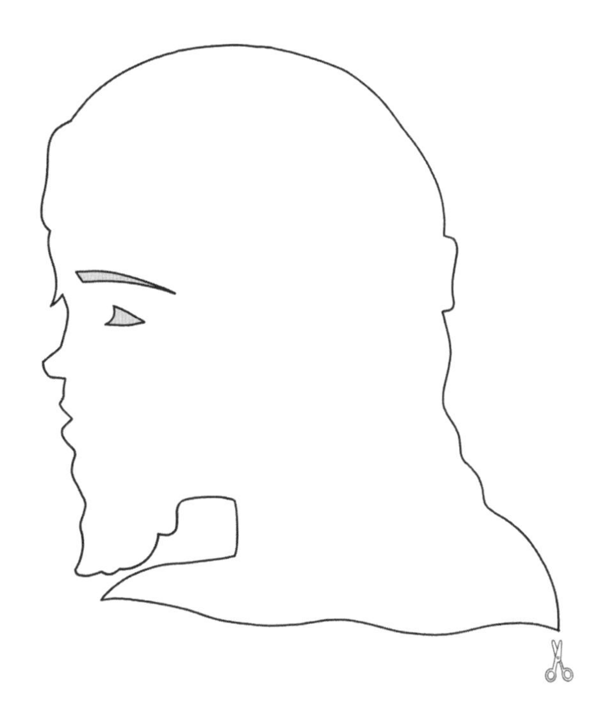

Face with half-closed eye

Angel with wings

Figure of a woman

Figure of Jesus

Flower shapes, leaf shapes

Bird shapes, butterfly shapes

Face masks

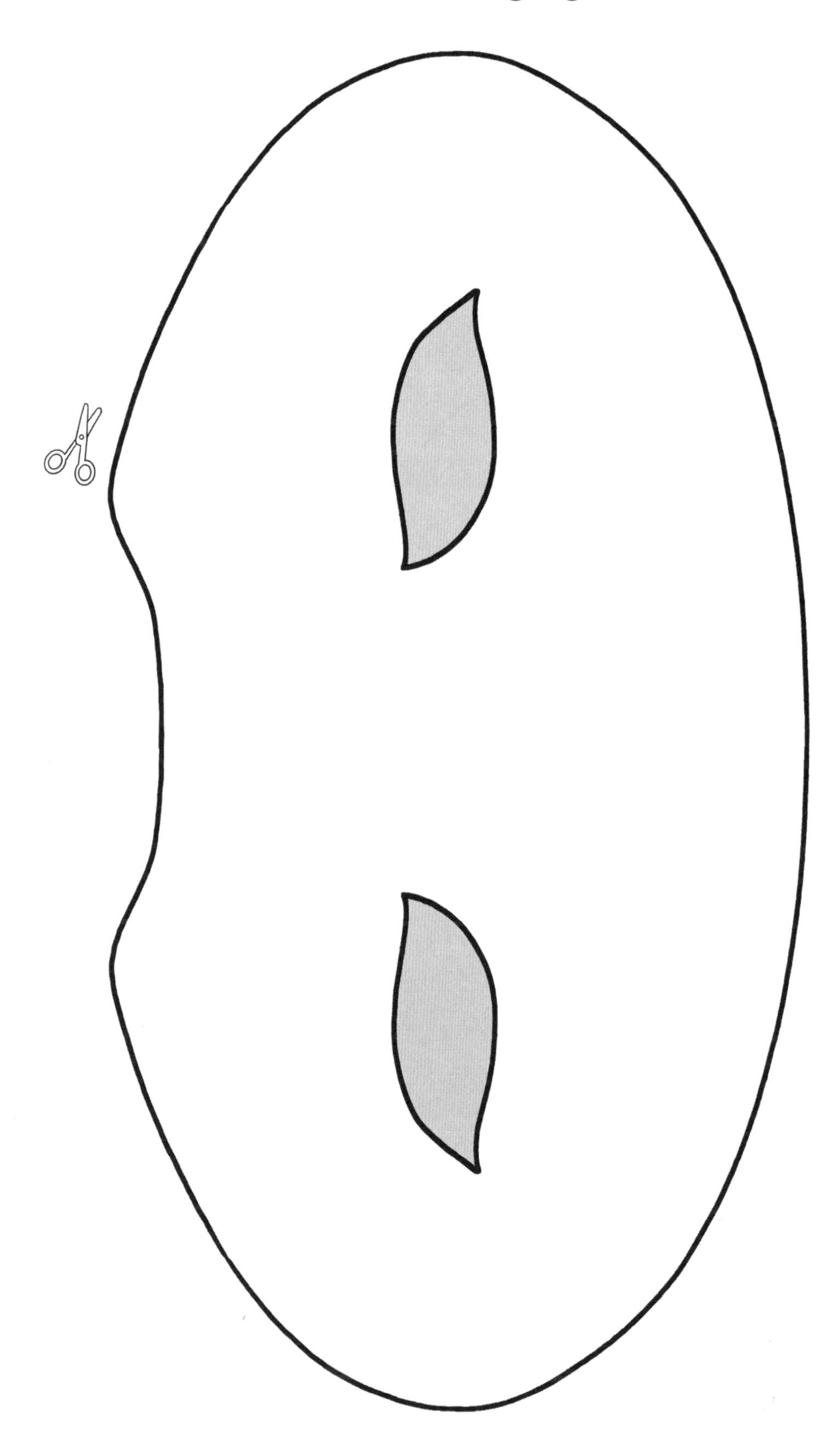